Letters from the Desert

ANNIVERSARY EDITION

Letters from the Desert

Carlo Carretto

Translated from Italian by Rose Mary Hancock

ORBIS BOOKS

Maryknoll, New York 10545

DARTON·LONGMAN + TODD

Founded in 1970, Orbis Books endeavors to publish works that enlighten the mind, nourish the spirit, and challenge the conscience. The publishing arm of the Maryknoll Fathers & Brothers, Orbis seeks to explore the global dimensions of the Christian faith and mission, to invite dialogue with diverse cultures and religious traditions, and to serve the cause of reconciliation and peace. The books published reflect the views of their authors and do not represent the official position of the Maryknoll Society. To learn more about Maryknoll and Orbis Books, please visit our website at www.maryknoll.org.

Published by Orbis Books, Maryknoll, NY 10545-0308, and Darton, Longman and Todd Ltd, 1 Spencer Court, 140–142 Wandsworth High Street, London SW18 4JJ.

Photographs courtesy of Maryknoll archives and the Little Brothers of the Gospel.

Originally published by La Scuola Editrice, Brescia, 1964.

First published in Great Britain in 1972. Second edition published 1990.

Manufactured in the United States of America

ORBIS/ISBN 1-57075-431-4
Cataloging-in-Publication Data is available from the Library of Congress, Washington, D.C.

DLT/ISBN 0-232-52471-8
A catalogue record for this book is available from the British Library.

Contents

FOREWORD

There are two kinds of deserts. The desolate wastelands, with their silences and overwhelming night skies, their hidden dangers, and the demands put on those who would enter them, have from time immemorial refined the great religious figures. Moses, Jesus, and Muhammad all experienced the revelatory experience of the wilderness. In our age we have also known another kind of desert—one that is constructed either by human malevolence (the gulags and the camps which dot our sorry history) or by human indifference and neglect (the slums and inner cities of our urban landscape).

It is the precise genius of the Little Brothers and Sisters of Jesus to have understood that one can be formed in the spirituality of the desert in order to live as a witness to the Gospel in the far more ominous deserts of urban sprawl. Inspired by the witness and writings of Charles de Foucauld (1858–1916), the Little Brothers and Sisters, founded in the 1930s, have made a desert spirituality of silent adoration adaptable for the postmodern society of slums and abandoned neighborhoods.

After an active, near frenetic, life as a schoolteacher and Catholic activist working at a national level in his native Italy, Carlo Carretto left his native land to embrace the life of a Little Brother in the deserts of North Africa. The letters he sent back were published in Italy in 1964 and, as a bestseller there, were translated and published in English in 1972. This new edition of *Letters from the Desert*, thirty years after their original publication, is testimony to the staying power of this profoundly powerful spiritual master who has known both national fame and religious obscurity.

How does one (re)read a book like this? The very contours of a desert spirituality—any Christian spirituality for that matter—provide the clues.

First, be prepared to listen to the voice behind the text. Carretto writes out of the matrix of prayer. What he writes comes with a wilderness background and so, paradoxically, we must listen both to what is said and to the silence behind the saying. In practical terms, that way of encounter demands that the work is to be read slowly and in small portions. In other words, this work should always be approached in the spirit of contemplative *lectio*. If Carretto asks a question we must be tolerant enough to attempt an answer. If he advances three ideas we need to take each one in turn. If he proffers a text from scripture we must take the opportunity to ruminate over it. Authentic prayer, after all, is as much a matter of listening as it is of speaking: "Oh, that today you would hear His voice/Harden not your heart . . ." (Ps 95:7–8).

Second, one must be prepared to respond with the same simplicity that he exhibits in writing. The desert experience pares things down and that resultant spareness applies to language as well. Many of the desert monastics made a single phrase—"Lord, be merciful to me a sinner"—the basis of a life-long prayer. Simple writing from the great spiritual masters can be deceptive in its simplicity. When Carretto tells us that "we are what we pray" there is an immense theological anthropology resting in that simple phrase which we will never "get" unless we are simple enough to see the truth toward which he points. When Carretto tells us that in prayer the night will be as clear as the day he is moving into the paradoxical realm of St. John of the Cross—a movement which is both utterly simple and deeply mysterious.

A classic, it has been said, is a work that has a surplus of meaning; it speaks from its own age and now spills over to nourish those of later times. *Letters from the Desert* is that kind of work. It is a book that comes from the pen of one person but its message is not confined to his time or his situation. After all, there is something primordial and fruitful in the message of someone who speaks compellingly of God not from mere speculation but from deep experience. Experience speaks in this work.

In the long history of Christian spirituality people built artificial deserts when it was no longer possible to live in an actual one. Carmelites live in constructed deserts and Cistercians today seek hermitages, as do so many others who feel the need for a quiet space for silence and prayer. Such constructed deserts often go under the name of solitude. It was Thomas Merton who taught us that solitude is not simply a matter of geography. All Christians need to find their desert if they wish to imitate the Christ who opened his ministry in one. The question, of course, is what kind of desert? It may be that circumstances have forced the need to find such a desert in our hearts, or it may be an actual desert in which we find our retreat. In either case, in the desert it is good to have a companion who has been there, who knows the way, who has surveyed the landscape and the silent canopy above. What better companion than Carlo Carretto; what better map than his *Letters from the Desert*?

LAWRENCE S. CUNNINGHAM
The University of Notre Dame

Introduction to the Anniversary Edition

In December 1954, at the age of forty-four, Carlo Carretto arrived in El Abiodh, a remote oasis in the Saharan desert of Algeria, to enter the novitiate of the Little Brothers of Jesus. For twenty years Carretto had served as a charismatic leader of the Italian youth movement of Catholic Action. At the peak of such an active and public career, Caretto's flight to the desert seemed a curious and puzzling move to many of his friends. In explanation Carretto himself could only say that he felt summoned by a call from God: "Leave everything and come with me into the desert. It is not your acts and deeds that I want: I want your prayer, your love."

Responding to this call, Carretto joined the Little Brothers and spent the next ten years as a desert hermit. As it turned out, however, the option for solitude hardly led to obscurity. The Italian publication in 1964 of *Letters from the Desert* established Carretto's reputation as one of the most popular religious voices in the world. With this edition, marking the thirtieth anniversary of the English translation, we are pleased to recognize the status of *Letters from the Desert* as a modern spiritual classic.

Carretto went on to write a dozen books, but it was *Letters from the Desert*, based directly on his experience in the desert, that most clearly summarized his message. As these meditations make clear, the flight to the desert was not an effort to spurn the "world" and its secular inhabitants. Instead, the desert was a school of love, a school of prayer, where Carretto learned to enter more deeply into the mystery of the God who, out of love, entered so intimately into our humanity. It was to share that message with his friends that he wrote this book.

In the pages that follow Carretto makes frequent reference to the example of Charles de Foucauld (1858–1916), the modern desert hermit whose life inspired the formation of the Little Brothers. Foucauld's great insight was that Jesus Christ, the Son of God, had been a poor man and a worker. As a carpenter in Nazareth he had, in these lowly circumstances, embodied the Gospel message in its entirety, before ever announcing it in words. On this basis Foucauld found his calling to live among the Muslim poor of North Africa and "preach the gospel with my life." And so too Carretto found the seeds of a new form of spiritual witness particularly adapted to the challenges of our age. Like St. Francis, whom he revered, Carretto believed urgently that the church must meet the world in the manner of its founder— without power, pomp, or privilege. It must show men and women how to find the way of holiness in the midst of work and everyday life. And it must lead the way in promoting peace and understanding between people of different races, religions, and cultures.

Apart from his reference to earlier saints and spiritual teachers, Carretto returns throughout these reflections to the lessons from his friends and neighbors in the desert—the ex-slaves, the nomads, the impoverished beggars who so often serve unwittingly as his guides in faith, hope, and charity. Often he returns to a poignant memory: his failure to give an extra blanket to a shivering beggar, and the subsequent day spent huddled in the shade of a precarious rock, meditating on his lack of charity. The desolate desert is no longer the paradise of solitude, but an image of purgatory, where he reflects that every circumstance, no matter how unforeseen, and every person, no matter how poor, harbors an invitation to communion with God. Thereon hangs our destiny and the meaning of our lives.

But the most important lesson Carretto learned in the Sahara was that nothing was to be gained from the search for God in the desert if it did not make it easier to find God in the midst of one's fellow human beings. Thus, in 1964, after writing this book, Carretto left the Sahara and returned to Europe. The next year he was asked to oversee a new experimental community, the Fraternity of St. Jerome, in Spello, Italy. There, in the Umbrian hills near Assisi, the Little Brothers had established a network of hermitages where lay people were invited to share, on a temporary basis, the fraternity's life of prayer and reflection. In these "hills of hope" as

Carretto called them, thousands of men and women over time were drawn to taste the spirituality of Charles de Foucauld. It was in this setting that Carretto went on to write his many popular books. And it was there, in 1988, after a long illness, that he died at the age of 78.

Carretto represented an ascetic, yet joy-filled spirituality available to lay people, even in the midst of pressing obligations, even amidst the din of city noise, even in the midst of poverty and suffering. He demonstrated that a life of prayer need not relieve one of a passion for social justice and a spirit of solidarity. At the same time he reminded social activists that in the midst of their good works they must preserve a place of stillness, a place where they can listen to the word of God, and find renewal. Essentially, Carretto showed that it is possible to live a contemplative life in the midst of the world—the desert, after all, is really everywhere. The heart of the Gospel, he believed, is to make of ourselves an oasis of love in whatever desert we might find ourselves. That was the challenge of his life, and it is the ultimate message of this book.

ROBERT ELLSBERG
Editor in Chief, Orbis Books

Preface

God's call is mysterious; it comes in the darkness of faith. It is so fine, so subtle, that it is only with the deepest silence within us that we can hear it.

And yet nothing is so decisive and overpowering for a man on this earth, nothing surer or stronger.

This call is uninterrupted: God is always calling us! But there are distinctive moments in this call of his, moments which leave a permanent mark on us— moments which we never forget.

Three times in my life I have been aware of this call.

The first one brought about my conversion when I was eighteen years old. I was a school-teacher in a country village.

In Lent a mission came to the town. I attended it but what I remember most of all was how boring and outdated the sermons were. It certainly wasn't the words which shook my state of apathy and sin. But when I knelt before an old missionary—I remember how direct his look was and how simple—I was aware that God was moving in the silence of my soul.

From that day on I knew I was a Christian, and was aware that a completely new life had been opened up for me.

The second time, when I was twenty-three, I was thinking of getting married. It never occurred to me that I should do anything else.

I met a doctor who spoke to me of the Church and of the beauty of serving her with one's whole being, while remaining in the world. I do not know what happened at that time nor how it happened; the fact is that I was praying in an empty church where I had gone to escape from my state of inner confusion. I heard the same voice that I had heard during my confession with the old missionary. "Marriage is not for you. You will offer your life to me. I shall be your Lover for ever."

I had no difficulty in giving up the idea of getting married and consecrating myself to God because everything within me was changed. It would have seemed incongruous to me, falling in love with a girl, for God engaged my whole life.

Those years were full of work, of aspirations, of meeting different people, and of wild dreams. Even the mistakes—and there were many—were caused by the fact that so much within me was still unpurified.

Many years passed; and many times I was amazed to find myself praying to hear once more the sound of that voice which had had so great an importance for me.

Then, when I was forty-four years old, there occurred the most serious call of my life: the call to the contemplative life. I experienced it deeply—in the depth which only faith can provide and where darkness is absolute— where human strength can no longer help.

This time I had to say "yes" without understanding a thing. "Leave everything and come with me into the desert. It is not your acts and deeds that I want; I want your prayer, your love."

Some people, seeing me leave for Africa, thought that I must have had some personal crisis, some disappointment. Nothing is further from the truth. By nature I am optimistic, my orientation is one of hope; and I don't know the meaning of discouragement and it would never occur to me to "give up the fight" in this way.

No, it was the decisive call. And I never understood it so deeply as on that evening at the Vespers of St. Charles in 1954, when I said "yes" to the voice.

"Come with me into the desert." There is something much greater than human action: prayer; and it has a power much stronger than human words: love.

And I went into the desert.

Without having read the constitutions of the Little Brothers of Jesus I entered their congregation. Without knowing Charles de Foucauld I began to follow him.

For me it was enough to have heard the voice say to me, "This is the way for you."

Wandering among the desert tracks with the Little Brothers I discovered how real that way was. By following Charles de Foucauld, I was convinced that it was the way for me.

God had already told me that in faith.

When I reached El Abiod Sidi Seik for the novitiate, my novice master told me with the perfect calm of a man who had lived twenty years in the desert: "*Il faut faire une coupure, Carlo.*" I knew what kind of cutting he was talking about and decided to make the wrench, even if it were painful.

In my bag I had kept a thick notebook, containing the addresses of my old friends: there were thousands of them. In his goodness God had never left me without the joys of friendship.

If there was one thing I really regretted when I left for Africa, it was not being able to speak to each one of them, to explain the reason for my abandoning them, to say that I was obeying a call from God and that, even if in a different way, I would continue to fight on with them to work for the Kingdom.

But it was necessary to make the "cut" and it demanded courage and great faith in God.

I took the address book, which for me was the last tie with the past, and burned it behind a dune during a day's retreat.

I can still see the black ashes of the notebook being swept away into the distance by the wind of the Sahara.

But burning an address is not the same thing as destroying a friendship, for that I never intended to do; on the contrary, I have never loved nor prayed so much for my old friends as in the solitude of the desert. I saw their faces, I felt their problems, their sufferings, sharpened by the distance between us.

For me they had become a flock which would always belong to me and which I must lead daily to the fountains of prayer.

Sometimes I almost felt their physical presence when, for example, I entered the Arab-style church at El Abiod or, later, the famous hermitage constructed by Fr. Charles de Foucauld himself at Tamanrasset.

Prayer had become the most important thing. But it was still the hardest part of my daily life. Through my vocation to prayer I learned what is meant by "carrying other people" in our prayer.

So, after many years I can say that I have remained true to my vocation, and at the same time I am completely convinced that one never wastes one's time by praying; there is no more helpful way of helping those we love.

The address book is mine no longer, but this is of no importance because there are other ways of reaching one's friends.

And so I'd like to make an appointment with you in one of the many wonderful corners of the Sahara toward evening at sunset.

Here there would be no need for torches, for the sky is so clear with stars.

We'd sit down on the sand and through the night we'd tell each other the story of these past years of our lives, of the stages we'd reached, and the trials we'd undergone. I think that the morning star would find us still talking.

For my part, in these "Letters from the Desert," I've tried to jot down the things I should say if such an opportunity were given me, and which of course represent part of myself.

Nothing systematic, nothing important. A few ideas matured in solitude and taking shape around an activity which has been, without any doubt, the greatest gift that the Sahara has given me: prayer.

CARLO CARRETTO

CHAPTER I

Under the Great Rock

THE TRACK, WHITE IN THE SUN, unwound ahead of me in a vague outline. The furrows in the sand made by the wheels of the great oil trucks forced me to keep alert every second, if I was to keep the jeep on the move.

The sun was high in the sky, and I felt tired. Only the wind blowing on the hood of the car allowed the jeep to continue, although the temperature was like hell-fire and the water was boiling in the radiator. Every now and then I fixed my gaze on the horizon. I knew that in the area there were great blocks of granite embedded in the sand: they provided highly desirable sources of shade under which to pitch camp and wait the evening before proceeding with the journey.

In fact, towards mid-day, I found what I was looking for. Great rocks appeared on the left of the track. I approached, in the hope that I would find a little shade. I was not disappointed. On the north wall of the thirty foot high slab of stone, a knife of shade was thrown on to the red sand. I pulled the jeep against the wind to cool the engine and unloaded the *ghess,* the necessary equipment for pitching camp: a bag of food, two blankets, and a tripod for the fire.

But approaching the rock I realized that in the shade there were some guests already there: two snakes were curled up in the warm sand, watching me motionlessly. I leapt backwards and retreated to the jeep without taking my eyes off the two serpents. I took the gun, an old contraption lent me by a native who used it to get rid of the jackals which, urged on by hunger and thirst, used to attack his flocks.

I loaded the gun, drew back a bit and took aim in order to try to hit the two snakes together, so as not to waste another bullet.

I fired, and saw the two beasts leap into the air in a cloud of sand. When I was cleaning up the blood and the remains of the snakes I saw, coming out of the mangled entrails of one of them, a bird he hadn't had time to digest. I spread out the mat. In the desert it is everything: chapel, dining-room, bedroom, drawing-room. It was the hour of Sext. I sat down, took out my breviary, and recited a few Psalms, but I had to force myself because I was so tired. Besides, every now and then the wind blew fragments of the two vipers I had killed onto the verses I was reading. Warm sultry air was coming from the south and my head ached. I got up. I calculated how much water I had to last me until I reached the well of Tit, and decided to sacrifice a little. From the goatskin gourd I drew a basinful of two pints and poured it on my head. The water soaked into my turban, ran down my neck and on to my clothes. The wind did the rest. From 115° the temperature descended in a few minutes to

80°. With that sense of refreshment I stretched out on the sand to sleep; in the desert you take your siesta before your meal.

In order to lie more comfortably I looked for a blanket to put under my head. I had two. One remained by my side unused, and as I looked at it I could not feel at ease.

But to understand you must hear my story.

The evening before I had passed through Irafog, a small village of Negroes, ex-slaves of the Tuareg. As usual when one reaches a village the people ran out to crowd round the jeep, either from curiosity, or to obtain the various things which desert-travellers bring with them: they may bring a little tea, distribute medicines or hand over letters.

That evening I had seen old Kada trembling with cold. It seems strange to speak of cold in the desert, but it is so; in fact the Sahara is often called "a cold country where it is very hot in the sun." The sun had gone down, and Kada was shivering. I had the idea of giving him one of the blankets I had with me, an essential part of my *ghess;* but I put the thought out of my mind. I thought of the night and I knew that I, too, would shiver. The little charity that was in me made me think again, though reasoning that my skin wasn't worth more than his and that I had best give him one of the blankets. Even if I shivered a little that was the least a Little Brother could do.

When I left the village the blankets were still on the jeep; and now they were giving me a bad conscience.

I tried to get to sleep with my feet resting on the great rock, but I couldn't manage it. I remembered that a month ago a Tuareg in the middle of his siesta had been crushed by a falling slab. I got up to make sure how stable the boulder was; I saw that it was a little off-balance, but not enough to be dangerous.

I lay down again on the sand. If I were to tell you what I dreamed of you would find it strange. The funny thing is that I dreamed that I was asleep under the great boulder and that at a given moment—it didn't seem to be a dream at all: I saw the rock moving, and I felt the boulder fall on top of me. What a nightmare! I felt my bones grating and I found myself dead. No, alive, but with my body crushed under the stone. I was amazed that not a bone hurt; but I could not move. I opened my eyes and saw Kada shivering in front of me at Irafog. I didn't hesitate for a minute to give him the blanket, especially as it was lying unused behind me, a yard away. I tried to stretch out my hand to offer it to him; but the stone made even the smallest movement impossible. I understood what purgatory was and that the suffering of the soul was "no longer to have the possibility of doing what before one could and should have done." Who knows for how many years afterwards I would be haunted by seeing that blanket near me as a witness to my selfishness and to the fact that I was too immature to enter the Kingdom of Love.

I tried to think of how long I was to remain under the rock. The reply was given me by the catechism:

"Until you are capable of an act of perfect love." At that moment I felt quite incapable.

The perfect act of love is Jesus going up to Calvary to die for us all. As a member of his Mystical Body I was being asked to show if I was close enough to that perfect love to follow my master to Calvary for the salvation of my brethren. The presence of the blanket denied to Kada the evening before told me that I had still a long way to go. If I were capable of passing by a brother who was shivering with cold, how should I be capable of dying for him in imitation of Jesus who died for us all? In this way I understood that I was lost, and that if somebody had not come to my aid, I should have lain there, aeon after aeon, without being able to move.

I looked away and realized that all those great rocks in the desert were nothing more than the tombs of other men. They too, judged according to their ability to love and found cold, were there to await him who once said, "I shall raise you up on the last day."

CHAPTER 2

You Will Be Judged by Love

EVEN NOW I COULD not tell you if the episode of the great rock were a dream, let alone what kind of dream. Its influence upon me has been so strong, my attitude towards things so changed by it, that I have never been able to describe it as what we commonly have in mind when we say upon waking, "I have had a dream."

No, for me that tract of desert between Tit and Silet is still the place of my purgatory, where I was forced to meditate seriously about the ways of God and where I shall probably ask to go after death to continue my expiation, if in life I have not been capable of performing an act of perfect love.

There is the great stone under the blinding sun of the Sahara, the slit of shade on the warm sand, the land up to the horizon furrowed with the marks of the oil trucks and the geologists' jeeps.

"You will be judged according to your ability to love," this place reminds me insistently. And my eyes, burnt by the sun, gaze up into the cloudless sky.

I don't want to deceive myself any more; indeed I am

not able to. The truth is that I did not give my blanket to Kada, for fear of the cold night. And that means that I love my own skin more than my brother's, while God's commandment tells me: "Love the life of others as you love your own."

And even that belongs to the Old Testament, to God's first revelation to humanity: "Love God above all things, and your neighbor as yourself" (Leviticus 19:18).

It's when we come to the New Testament and the revelation of Jesus that things get more complicated. "Love one another. Just as I have loved you, you must also love one another" (John 13:34).

As I have loved you. This is not only to give up the blanket, but life itself. The perfect act of love consists in being ready to do what Jesus did: he died for Kada, for me, for everybody. Seen in this way, heaven is that place where everyone must be so mature in love as to offer his life for all others. It is love which is universal, and lies at the heart of things; where every vestige of hate, resentment and selfishness has been destroyed by this love and cast into its fire.

And so, after the vision of the great rock, I expect my purgatory to be long, terribly long, perhaps as long as the geological eras. This sand which I am touching with my hands and which is running through my fingers, belongs to the "first era." Any geologist will tell me that it is 350 million years old. The great reptiles that inhabited these regions, whose remains I have seen in Sahara ditches, belong to the second era: 130 million years ago.

Those camels which carry the salt of the Niger and are passing in front of me in long well-ordered caravans have their ancestors in the distant third period: 70 million years ago. And human beings, at once so tiny and so great, how slowly we advance upon the remains of the animals which have preceded us. We are of the fourth era, of yesterday: 500,000 years ago.

God does not hurry over things; time is his, not mine. And I, little creature, a man, have been called to be transformed into God by sharing his life. And what transforms me is the charity which he pours into my heart.

Love transforms me slowly into God.

But sin is still there, resisting this transformation, knowing how to, and actually saying "no" to love.

Living in our selfishness means stopping at human limits and preventing our transformation into Divine Love. And until I am transformed, sharing the life of God, through love, I shall be of "this earth" and not of "that heaven." Baptism has raised me to the supernatural state, but we must grow in this state, and the purpose of life is precisely that growth. And charity, or rather God's love, is what transforms us.

To have resisted love, not to have been capable of accepting the demand of this love which said to me, "Give the blanket to your brother," is so serious that it creates an obstacle between me and God and this is my purgatory.

What's the use of saying the Divine Office well, of sharing the Eucharist, if one is not impelled by love?

What's the use of giving up everything and coming here to the desert and the heat, if only to resist love?

What's the good of defending the truth, fighting over dogmas with the theologians, getting shocked at those who haven't the same faith and then living purgatory for geological epochs?

"You will be judged according to your ability to love," says the great stone under which I spent my purgatory waiting for perfect love to grow within myself, that which Jesus brought to earth for me, and gave me at the price of his blood, shot through with the great cry of hope, "I shall raise you up at the last day" (John 6:40).

May that day be not far off.

CHAPTER 3

You Are Nothing

THE GREAT JOY of the Saharan novitiate is the solitude, and the joy of solitude—silence, true silence, which penetrates everywhere and invades one's whole being, speaking to the soul with wonderful new strength unknown to men to whom this silence means nothing.

Here, living in perpetual silence, one learns to distinguish its different shades: silence of the church, silence in one's cell, silence at work, interior silence, silence of the soul, God's silence.

To learn to live these silences, the novice-master lets us go away for a few days' 'desert.'

A hamper of bread, a few dates, some water, the Bible. A day's march: a cave.

A priest celebrates Mass, then goes away, leaving in the cave, on an altar of stones, the Eucharist. Thus, for a week one remains alone with the Eucharist exposed day and night. Silence in the desert, silence in the cave, silence in the Eucharist. No prayer is so difficult as the adoration of the Eucharist. One's whole natural strength rebels against it.

One would prefer to carry stones in the sun. The

senses, memory, imagination, all are repressed. Faith alone triumphs, and faith is hard, dark, stark.

To place oneself before what seems to be bread and to say, "Christ is there living and true," is pure faith.

But nothing is more nourishing than pure faith, and prayer in faith is real prayer.

"There's no pleasure in adoring the Eucharist," one novice used to say to me. But it is precisely this renunciation of all desire to satisfy the senses that makes prayer strong and real. One meets God beyond the senses, beyond the imagination, beyond nature.

This is crucial: as long as we pray only when and how we want to, our life of prayer is bound to be unreal. It will run in fits and starts. The slightest upset—even a toothache—will be enough to destroy the whole edifice of our prayer-life.

"You must strip your prayers," the novice-master told me. You must simplify, deintellectualize. Put yourself in front of Jesus as a poor man: not with any big ideas, but with living faith. Remain motionless in an act of love before the Father. Don't try to reach God with your understanding; that is impossible. Reach him in love; that is possible.

The struggle is not easy, because nature will try to get back her own, get her dose of enjoyment; but union with Christ Crucified is something quite different.

After some hours—or some days—of this exercise, the body relaxes. As the will refuses to let it have its own way it gives up the struggle. It becomes passive. The senses go to sleep. Or rather, as St. John of the Cross says, the night of senses is beginning. Then prayer becomes something serious, even if it is painful and dry. So serious that one can no longer do without it. The soul begins to share the redemptive work of Jesus.

Kneeling down on the sand before the simple monstrance which contained Jesus, I used to think of the evils of the world: hate, violence, depravity, impurity, egoism, betrayal, idolatry. Around me the cave had become as large as the world, and inwardly I contemplated Jesus oppressed under the weight of so much wickedness.

Is not the Host in its own form like bread crushed, pounded, baked? And does it not contain the Man of Sorrows, Christ the Victim, the Lamb slain for our sins?

And what was my relationship to him?

For many years I had thought I was "somebody" in the Church. I had even imagined this sacred living structure of the Church as a temple sustained by many columns, large and small, each one with the shoulder of a Christian under it.

My own shoulder too I thought of as supporting a column, however small.

Through repeating that God needed men and the Church needed activists, we believed it.

The structure was a burden on our shoulders.

After creating the world, God went away to rest; with the Church founded, Christ had disappeared into heaven. All the work remained for us, the Church. We, above all those in Catholic Action, were the real workers, who bore the weight of the day.

With this mentality I was no longer capable of taking a holiday; even during the night I felt I was "in action." There was never enough time to get everything done. One raced continually from one project to another, from one meeting to another, from one city to another. Prayer was hurried, conversations frenzied, and one's heart in a turmoil.

As everything depended on us, and everything was going so badly, we were quite right to be worried.

But who noticed that? So convinced were we that the path of action was right, was true.

Even from childhood we began with the motto: "Be first in everything for the honor of Christ the King"; then, as teenagers "You must show the way"; and when we were adults, "You are a person of responsibility, a leader, an apostle." The soul always had to be "something"; the words of Jesus: "You are unprofitable servants, without me you can do nothing," "Whichever of you want to be first shall be last," seemed to have been said to other people, people of another age. They flowed over our heads without leaving much impression on us; they flowed over the heart without affecting it in any way, without bathing it, softening it.

My first master had told me, "The beginning of everything should be the honor of Christ the King"; the last, Charles de Foucauld, had advised me: "The end of everything is the love of Jesus Crucified."

And yet perhaps both of them were right, and the guilty one was I, for not understanding the lesson properly.

In any case, now I was here, kneeling on the sand of the cave, which had taken on the dimensions of the Church itself; on my shoulders I could feel the small column of the activist. Perhaps this was the moment of truth.

I drew back suddenly, as though to free myself from this weight. What had happened? Everything remained in its place, motionless. Not a movement, not a sound. After twenty-five years I had realized that nothing was burdening my shoulders and that the column was my own creation—sham, unreal, the product of my imagination and my vanity.

I had walked, run, spoken, organized, worked, in the belief that I was supporting something; and in reality I had been holding up absolutely nothing.

The weight of the world was all on Christ Crucified. I was nothing, absolutely nothing.

It had taken some effort to believe the words of Jesus who had said to me two thousand years earlier: "When you have done everything that is commanded you to do, say, 'We are unprofitable servants, because we have only done our duty'" (Luke 17:10).

Unprofitable servants!

Chapter 4

Who Guides the World?

My first feeling after this was one of freedom; new, vast, real, joyful freedom.

The discovery that I was nothing, that I was responsible for no one, that I was a man of no importance, gave me the joy of a boy on holiday.

Night came, and I could not sleep. I left the cave, and walked under the stars above the vast desert.

"My God, I love you. My God, I love you," I shouted to the heavens through the strange silence of the night.

Tired of walking, I stretched out on a sand dune and gazed at the starry vault above. How dear they were to me, those stars; how close to them the desert had brought me. Through spending my nights in the open, I had come to know them by their names, then to study them, and to get to know them one by one. Now I could distinguish their color, their size, their position, their beauty. I knew my way around them, and from them I could calculate the time without a watch. The constellation of the Swan seemed to be in conversation with Altair which was as clear as a diamond. Confined by their smallness, Sagitta and the Dolphin seemed to be listening. Pegasus was rising in the East with his entourage of stars, while the Pearl was disappearing into the West.

I cast my eyes back to Andromeda. The night was so clear that I could just discern the nebula that bears the name of the constellation. It is the celestial body which is farthest from the Earth yet visible to the naked eye: 800 thousand light years away. Between them and the Earth is Proxina, the four light-years of which would appear to me in two months' time in the constellation of Centaurus. Such is the space occupied by this mass of forty million stars in which is gathered the galaxy to which we belong—on a tiny grain of sand called Earth.

Beyond the nebula Andromeda are other millions of nebulae, and thousands and thousands of stars which my eyes cannot see, but which God has created.

It is true that Jesus said, "Go, and make disciples of all nations." But he also added, "Without me you can do nothing." It is true that Saint Ignatius said, "Act as though everything depended upon you." But he added, "But pray as though everything depended upon God." God is the creator of the physical cosmos as well as of the human cosmos. He rules the stars as he rules the Church. And if, in his love, he has wished to make men and women his collaborators in the work of salvation, the limit of their power is very small and clearly defined. It is the limit of the wire compared with the electric current.

We are the wire, God is the current. Our only power is to let the current pass through us. Of course, we have the power to interrupt it and say "no." But nothing more.

Not, then, the image of the column acting as a support, but that of the wire allowing the current to pass through it.

But the wire is one thing, the current is another. They are quite different, and there is certainly no reason for the wire to become self-satisfied, even one which transmits at high tension.

The thought that the affairs of the world, like those of the stars, are in God's hands—and therefore in good hands—apart from being actually true, is something that should give great satisfaction to anyone who looks to the future with hope. It should be the source of faith, joyful hope, and, above all, of deep peace. What have I to fear if everything is guided and sustained by God? Why get so worried, as if the world were in the hands of me and my fellow humans?

And yet it is so difficult to have genuine faith in God's action in the affairs of the world. To refuse to believe it is one of the gravest temptations to which we are subjected on this earth.

The whole Bible is there to testify to this fact. And basically the story of the chosen people is nothing more than that of a handful of men of whom God asks, time and time again:

Do you believe in me? I am the God of Abraham and of Isaac and Jacob. I am the God who with a strong arm has brought you out of the slavery of Egypt, and guided you into a parched land. I have nourished you with bread from Heaven and I have given you to drink water gushing out of the rock. For you I have stricken the first-born of Egypt, for you I have struck down many kings. And what have you done to pay me for all these wonders, for this continual help? You have constructed for yourselves idols of wood and silver, and have abandoned me, your God.

Instead of worshipping Him who has created you and saved you a thousand times from your enemies, on the hill-tops and in sacred woods, you have burnt incense to strange gods; gods who can do nothing and know nothing; who have hands and cannot touch, feet and cannot walk, and no sound comes from their mouths.

This is true of all time, of the history of Israel and of our history. We too believe in God. But then we put our trust in men of power, believe their advice, and in the end think that the affairs of this world are safe in their hands, and that it is to them we must make our petitions. We too believe in God and we pray to him. But then we convince ourselves that it is the great preachers who convert souls. And if we have this in mind when we pray for the growth of the Kingdom our prayer will be futile; like making a request which will almost certainly be ignored.

And so, under a strange sky, the poor life of our soul goes on, in the light of unreal faith and sentimentalism. Halfway between God and the world there is a confusion of aspirations, contradictions and compromises.

Only God is, only God knows, only God can do anything. This is the truth, and with the help of my faith I discover this more deeply every day.

God alone rules the cosmos, only God knows when I shall die, only God can convert China.

Why try to take on responsibilities that are not ours, why be amazed if Islam has not yet discovered Christ, or if millions of our brethren adhere to Buddhism, and are spiritually satisfied? The hour will come, but that in no way depends on me.

Does God have a plan for the world, a sacred history for all peoples? Is there an advance in time towards some goal?

Abraham did not know Christ, except in the hope of the promise. But this was no reason for him to be lost, or forgotten by the Father. The moment for the Incarnation had not come; and if Jesus came when he came and not before, it was certainly all part of the Divine Wisdom. God's plans count. Human plans count only in so far as they synchronize with God's.

God comes first, not humans. Mary herself could have died without seeing Christ, had God not decided that the moment for the Incarnation had come.

The men of Galilee would have gone on fishing in the lake and attending the synagogue of Capernaum if he hadn't been there to say "Come." That is the truth we must learn through faith: to wait on God. And this attitude of mind is not easy. This "waiting," this "not making plans," this "searching the heavens," this "being silent" is one of the most important things we have to learn.

The moment will then follow when we are called, when we must speak out, when our hands will have grown tired from baptizing: the moment of the harvest. But even then we will be blind if we think of ourselves as the sole agents in bringing it about. The extraordinary thing is that God uses us, who are so insignificant and unworthy.

I didn't want to reach this point, because there is a question I am loathe to tackle. Even to ask the question seems impertinent, and lacking in faith.

"Pray or act? Stay or opt out? Go out into the world or use the Church as a refuge?" And there we are at the beginning again, where man persists in posing irrelevant questions. His hankering curiosity is so much stronger than his desire to obey the word of God.

But now I'm tired of arguing. I don't want to go on disputing any more. My belief in the ability to convince by words alone has gone.

I am silent under these African stars, and I prefer to worship my God and Savior.

But I must react in some way to the insistence of the young people who have written to me here; they do put their finger on an important point, and what is more, they have suffered. I can reply only that in the world everything is problematic except one thing: charity, love. Love alone is not a problem for him who lives it.

I can only say, "Live love, let love invade you. It will never fail to teach you what you must do."

Charity, which is God in us, will point to the way ahead. It will say to you "Now kneel," or "Now leave."

It is love which gives things their value. It makes sense of the difficulty of spending hours and hours on one's knees praying while so many need looking after in the world; and in the context of love we must view our inability to change the world, to wipe out evil and suffering.

It is love which must determine one's actions, love which must give unity to what is divided.

Love is the synthesis of contemplation and action, the meeting-point between heaven and earth, between God and humanity.

I have known the satisfaction of unrestrained action, and the joy of the contemplative life in the dazzling peace of the desert, and I repeat again St. Augustine's words: "Love and do as you will." Don't worry about what you ought to do. Worry about loving. Don't interrogate heaven repeatedly and uselessly saying, "What course of action should I pursue?" Concentrate on loving instead.

And by loving you will find out what is for you. Loving, you will listen to the Voice. Loving, you will find peace.

Love is the fulfillment of the law and should be everyone's rule of life; in the end it's the solution to every problem, the motive for all good.

"Love and do as you will."

This is the crux. When I love I can no longer do as I will.

When I love I am love's prisoner; and love is tremendous in its demands when it has God as its object, especially a crucified God. I can no longer do my own will. I *must* do the will of Jesus, which is the will of the Father.

And when I have learned to do his will, I shall have fully realized my vocation on earth and I shall have achieved the highest stage a man can reach.

The will of God. That's what rules the world and moves the stars, what converts the nations, what starts all life and brings triumph out of death.

The will of God raised up Abraham, our father in faith; it called Moses, inspired David, prepared Mary, sustained Joseph, made Christ incarnate and demanded his sacrifice; this it was that founded the Church. And it is God's will still to continue the work of redemption until the end of time.

It will call people to enter one by one into the visible body of the Church when the time is ripe after having belonged to his invisible soul through their good intentions and good will. Whether you are on the sand worshipping, or at the teacher's desk in a classroom, what does it matter as long as you are doing the will of God?

And if the will of God urges you to seek out the poor, to give up all you possess, or to leave for distant lands, what does the rest matter? Or if it calls you to found a family, or take on a job in a city, why should you have any doubts?

"His will is our peace," says Dante. And perhaps that is the expression which best brings into focus our deep dependence on God.

Chapter 5

Purification of the Heart

IT IS CLEAR WE ARE made to love. The difficulty is to establish what to love and how.

I don't think it is mistaken or contrary to our aims to "love a creature." And it is certainly according to our aims to "love Christ." Therefore we must love both creature and creator. But why in the Christian tradition are these two loves often placed in mutual opposition, almost as though love of the one made love of the other impossible? The reason must be found in ourselves. It is our heart which is no longer capable of loving. It is like a rusty machine that won't work properly.

The heart, with all its potential, loses its balance too easily when it loves a creature.

It throws itself upon the creature loved and wants to possess it; and possessiveness kills. It holds on to the creature so passionately that it loses sight of the creator.

Moreover it ruins the object of its love by its obsession with it. It ruins it, makes it a slave. Characteristic in this sense, because it is more violent, is the love of sex for its own sake, with all the jealousy and selfishness that entails. Equally characteristic is the so-called blind devotion in which the human heart attaches itself exclusively to another, losing its peace, its serenity, its balanced vision of things, and in the worst cases its purity.

What should we say then of the love of money? Of the slavery in which man is held by the love of riches?

Even love of work may become dangerous, especially if it is hidden behind a facade of virtue. There are so many country-people who are no longer capable of taking a rest on Sundays! Their obsession with goods and profit drives them into the fields.

And how many in business make a hell out of their lives, sucked in by the machine of their "obligations."

The higher one rises the worse it is. Even the love of study can make people unbelievably selfish; the passion for research can make men as mad and blind as termites in their dark tunnel. In situations such as these, it is clear that the love of creatures is an obstacle to the love of God.

The love of God is by nature pure, balanced and holy. Whoever is dominated by it lives in deep peace, has an ordered view of things and knows the meaning of true freedom. But the love of God, too, passing into one's heart, must be worked at, cultivated, pruned, fertilized. And the most uncompromising farmer is God Himself.

Above all such love must be purified.

What does it mean, to purify love?

It means releasing love from the fetters of the senses and from the pursuit of pleasure. In other words, making it free to grow in our hearts.

Freeing the gift of love! What a difficult undertaking for creatures like ourselves, willingly trapped as we are by sin, shut in by our selfishness.

We often fail to realize the depth of evil, terrifying as it is. I am not speaking only of the selfishness of the wealthy, heaping up riches for themselves, or of those who sacrifice to achieve their self-selected goals. Or of the dictator who breathes in the incense due only to God.

I am speaking of the selfishness of good people, devout people, those who have succeeded through spiritual exercises and self-denial in being able to make the proud profession before the altar of the Most High, "Lord, I am not like the rest of men." Yes, we have had the audacity at certain times of our lives to believe we are different from other men. And here is the deepest form of self-deception, dictated by self-centeredness at its worst: spiritual egotism. This most insidious form of egotism even uses piety and prayer for its own gain.

This becomes a form of insult to the altar itself. It is when the very desire for holiness itself is turned upside down. It is not love and imitation of Christ Crucified, it is the desire for glory. It is not charity, it is egotism.

I believe very strongly that a large proportion of the good intentions which drive us on to seek God are ruined in this way. One can reach the point of consecrating oneself to God for egotistic motives, becoming a religious for that reason, building hospitals, doing all kinds of good works.

There is no limit to such self-deception. And the path, once entered upon, is so slippery that God has to treat us harshly to bring us back to our senses.

But there is no other way of opening our eyes. It has to be painful.

But often it isn't enough. Disaster, illness, disappointment hover like birds of prey over the poor carcass that had the temerity to say, "Lord, I am not like the rest of men."

How can we possibly entertain the idea that we are different from other men, when we shout, cry, feel afraid, lack determination, and behave atrociously just like everybody else?

> Yahweh my God, I call for help all day,
> I weep to you all night;
> for my soul is all troubled,
> my life is on the brink of Sheol;
> I am numbered among those who go
> down to the pit,
> a man bereft of strength:
> You have plunged me to the bottom of the pit,
> to its darkest, deepest place,
> weighed down by your anger,
> drowned beneath your waves. (Ps. 88)

It is the purification of love, the refining fire which exposes our nakedness.

And God himself, who is love, is not powerless.

On the contrary, because he is love, he acts with greater determination.

If the soul does not free itself by way of the cross it can never be free. It is the tremendous surgical operation which the Father himself carries out on the flesh of his son in order to save him. And it is a dogma of faith that without the cross "there is no forgiveness." A mystery, but it is so. Pain purifies love. It makes it true, real, pure. And in addition it gets rid of what is not really love. It frees love from pleasure which falsifies it like a mask. It makes it a gift freely given.

When the flood of pain has passed over the soul, what remains alive can be considered genuine. Certainly not much remains. Often it is reduced to a thin shrub. But on this the dove of the Holy Spirit may rest to pour out his grace. It is reduced to a "yes" murmured among tears and anguish, but echoed by the all-powerful "yes" of the dying Jesus; it is reduced to a child who has ceased to argue with God and humans, but is helped on by the kiss of the Father.

In this state the soul is capable of a love which is freely given. It can no longer bear any other kind of love. It feels nausea when faced with sentiment. It loathes calculated love. It has finally entered into the logic of God, so often illogical to men and women of this earth.

Let us consider the logic of the most famous parable on the nature of true love:

The kingdom of Heaven is like a householder who went out early in the morning to hire laborers for his vineyard. After agreeing with the laborers for a denarius a day, he sent them into his vineyard. And going out about the third hour he saw others standing idle in the market place; and to them he said, "You go into the vineyard too, and whatever is right I will give you." So they went. Going out again about the sixth hour and the ninth hour he did the same. And about the eleventh hour he went out and found others standing; and he said to them, "Why do you stand here idle all day?" They said to him, "Because no one has hired us." He said to them, "You go into the vineyard too." And when evening came the owner said to his steward, "Call the laborers and pay them their wages, beginning with the last, up to the first." And when those hired about the eleventh hour came, each of them received a denarius. Now when the first came, they thought they would receive more; but each of them also received a denarius. And on receiving it they grumbled at the householder, saying, "These last worked only one hour, and you have made them equal to us who have borne the burden of the day and the scorching heat." But he replied to one of them, "Friend, I am doing you no wrong; did you not agree with me for a denarius? Take what belongs to you and go; I chose to give to this last as I give to you. Am I not allowed to do what I choose with what belongs to me? Or is your eye evil because I am good?" (Matthew 20:1–16)

Understanding this parable for us who have an "evil eye" is not easy. Anyone who understands it just a little before dying is blessed. For it means that now one's eye sees straight and thus one can enter into the kingdom of freedom which is the kingdom of a love which is real and unqualified.

CHAPTER 6

Toward Prayer

I HAVE COME into the desert to pray, to learn to pray. It has been the Sahara's great gift to me, and I should like to share it with all my friends. It is immeasurable and contains every other gift within itself. It is the *sine qua non* of life, the treasure buried in the field, the pearl of great price discovered in the market.

Prayer is the sum of our relationship with God.

We are what we pray.

The degree of our faith is the degree of our prayer. The strength of our hope is the strength of our prayer. The warmth of our charity is the warmth of our prayer. No more nor less.

Our prayer has had a beginning because we have had a beginning. But it will have no end. It will accompany us into eternity and will be completed in our contemplation of God, when we join in the harmony of heaven and are "filled with the flood of God's delights."

The story of our earthly-heavenly life will be the story of our prayer. Thus, above all it is a personal story.

Just as no flower is exactly like another flower, and no star exactly like another star, so no person is exactly like another. And since prayer is the relationship between one particular person and God, it is different for everyone. So no prayer is exactly like another.

Prayer is a word of infinite variety, were it repeated into infinity with the same syllables and in the same tone of voice.

What varies is the Spirit of the Lord which gives it life, and this is always new.

St. Bernadette Soubirous, who couldn't say anything but "Ave Maria" and the mystic who can only repeat one monosyllable, "God," have both the most variable and personal prayer imaginable.

Under the veil of the single word passes alone and entire the Spirit of Jesus, which is the Spirit of the Father.

Understanding prayer well means understanding that one is speaking with God.

Thus there are two poles. One very, very tiny and very, very weak: my soul. One immense and powerful: God.

But here is the first paradox, the first surprise: that he who is so great should have wanted to speak to me, tiny as I am.

It is not I who wanted prayer. It is he who wanted it. It is not I who have looked for him. It is he who has looked for me first. My seeking him would have been in vain if before all time he had not sought me.

The hope on which my prayer rests is in the fact that it is he who wants it. And if I go to keep the appointment it is because he is already there waiting for me.

If he had remained in his silence and isolation, I'd not have been able to break mine. Nobody has ever concentrated for long on talking to a wall or a tree or a star. He'd have given it up very soon if he didn't get a reply.

I've been speaking with God all my life; and I've only just begun!

There's another thing to say about prayer. It doesn't come from earth but from heaven. The cry which fills my breast and makes me exclaim, "God, I love you!"; the force which makes Farragi, the blind Muslim, repeat as he walks on the track at my side, "How great God is!"; the cry of David, "Have mercy!"; the exaltation of Mary, "Magnificat!"; the tear sparkling in the penitent's eye, "Jesus have mercy on me!"; the sudden ecstatic gasp of the scientist before the wonders of the universe, all these are the words of the Holy Spirit.

It is the Holy Spirit who fills the world and makes us cry "Father," and inspires the current of prayer within us. We should respond quickly with our lips and our hearts, full of awareness of the passage of God's current. We should repeat again and again what the Spirit of Jesus has prompted us and given us the strength to say. Certainly we can resist him, as we do most of the time. We can close our lips and be silent. If we were attentive to the call we should be in continual prayer.

To be precise, we must add there's a prayer we can call ours, that is, born on earth in the human heart. But there's nothing special about this prayer. Often it's a bit of spiritual pettiness: asking for things which aren't for our real good and which would be bad for us if they were granted to us, filling our mouths with pious words of fear, of loneliness or pain. Jesus had already warned us of this: "When you pray, do not do as the heathen do. . . ." If we wish for a comparison between the value of this prayer (let's call it 'not inspired') and the other true one dictated in us by the Spirit of the Lord, let's say that the difference between the two is like the difference between what philosophers have said about God, and what the Bible and the Church have said about him. After endless argument and deliberation the philosophers hardly succeeded in agreeing on the existence of God. The Church has a warm, living, spiritual knowledge of God even if it is obscure and hidden in the "darkness" of faith.

In any case there's no point in concerning ourselves with "our" prayer. We know it well.

How often we have been found with our mouths full of it, far from the Spirit of God! How often we've taken refuge in it precisely to escape the Spirit of God and his Will!

We have gone into choir to recite our breviary, while our duty was to go into the parlor to receive some tedious, grumpy bore. We have said the rosary while going to keep an appointment which could only cause harm to our soul. We have lit a candle and asked for money. We have bent our heads in adoration while our hearts were full of impure love.

This prayer comes from earth, not heaven. And on earth it remains, rich only in its uselessness, its deceit.

The Prophet will say of it, "I shall put clouds to stop it."

But I don't think even clouds are necessary, because it goes no further than the hearts of our blind obstinacy.

Yes, blind obstinacy that can last years. It creates in us a deep-seated hypocrisy which dominates every aspect of our daily lives. A man can go to Mass daily and proceed to exploit the poor; a man who is basically selfish can have his head crammed with ideas for reforming the Church.

Basically the answer is simple, very simple. We need only to listen to what Jesus has told us. It's enough to listen to the Gospel and put into practice what it tells us.

In short, it's the will that counts, not words.

God's inspiration searches out our will. The spirit of Jesus settles where the will desires it, because it is love. And two are needed to make love.

When I bow before his love he is not slow to come; rather he has already come, for he loves me much more than I, poor creature, can ever love him.

And love shows itself in action, as for the Prodigal Son.

Rising up is a fact, leaving the pigs is a fact.

The soul must say with sincerity, "Now I will arise and go to my Father."

CHAPTER 7

The Stages of Prayer

PRAYER IS WORDS, poetry, song.

> Turn your ear, O Lord, and give answer
> For I am poor and needy.
> Show me, Lord, your way,
> so that I may walk in thy truth
> Guide my heart to fear your name. (Ps. 86)

Often it contains a shout, a cry, a groan of anguish.

> Lord my God, I call for help by day;
> I cry at night before you.
> Let my prayer come into your presence.
> O turn your ear to my cry.
>
> For my soul is filled with evils;
> my life is on the brink of the grave.
> I am reckoned as one in the tomb:
> I have reached the end of my strength,
> like one alone among the dead;
> like the slain lying in their graves;
> like those you remember no more,
> cut off, as they are, from your hand. (Ps. 88)

And sometimes an explosion of joy:

> I love you, Lord, my strength,
> My rock, my fortress, my savior.
> My God is the rock where I take refuge. (Ps. 18)

Or ecstatic admiration of God's works:

> The heavens proclaim the glory of God
> And the firmament shows forth
> the work of his hands. (Ps. 19)

Or the impassioned praise of His providence:

> The Lord is my shepherd;
> There is nothing I shall want.
> Fresh and green are the pastures
> Where He gives me repose.
> He guides me along the right path;
> He is true to his name.
> If I should walk in the valley of darkness
> no evil would I fear.
> You are there with your crook
> and your staff;
> And with these you give me comfort. (Ps. 23)

This way of speaking to God is for people of all ages and cultures. People will express themselves in those ways from the beginning of their spiritual life until the end. With words they will express their feelings to their creator.

But here too, it is the same as with love. Words pour out to begin with. Then they get rarer and deeper. In the end they are reduced to some monosyllable which none the less contains everything. Mostly a soul speaks a great deal at the time of its conversion, during the period of its novitiate, that is, the first years of its discovery of God. It is the easiest time for the soul. Prayer has a certain novelty, it seizes the imagination. And God, for his part, encourages the soul; everything pours out as in the beginning of a happy marriage.

> My heart is ready, O God;
> I will sing, sing your praise.
> Awake, my soul;
> awake, lyre and harp.
> I will awake the dawn.
>
> I will thank you, Lord among the peoples,
> Praise you among the nations;
> for your love reaches to the heavens
> and your truth to the skies. (Ps. 108)

Another stage of prayer is meditation. Sometimes it naturally follows the use of words. Especially when the soul is mature, the two become blended and fused. Sometimes meditation comes later.

We are now at the stage when we need to know what

others have said about God; the stage of deep reflection, and of theological study; it is very, very rewarding.

If the world knew the joy Christians feel at this time, the peace which reigns in their hearts, and the sense of balance which dominates their whole being, it would be intrigued, fascinated.

I have known this and I have had the good fortune to share it with hundreds, thousands of other young people. God, the Church, souls, were the only enthusiasms we had. It seemed everyday we had a new world to forge. We moved against error like David against Goliath. A number of us met together to pray and speak of God. What did they matter, those sleepless nights, those long train journeys on wooden benches, those treks across the countryside by bicycle to spread our movement; the economic sacrifices and the holidays we gave up so that once a year we could make a retreat? These are among the dearest memories of my life and I always recall them with joy and peace.

There are a thousand ways of meditating, and everyone must find what suits him best. We will realize, as we go on, which way is the most suitable for us. Here I would like to mention two things which I have learned from my great master, John of the Cross—one on the method of meditation, and the other on the book to choose.

The Method: Saint John divides it into three parts, and up to this point there's nothing new.

1. Imaginative reflection on the mystery which one wishes to meditate.

2. Intellectual consideration of the mysteries represented. (Here too there's nothing new).

3. (And this is important.) Loving and attentive repose in God, to make sure we are fully prepared for that moment when the intelligence opens itself up to God's illumination.

This exercise of love, which is deeply human, results in a serene and devout repose before God. It must be meditation clearly directed towards simplicity and interior silence.

The Book to Chose: Above all other books, choose the Bible. If you like, read as many books of meditation as possible, but that isn't essential. It is essential to read and meditate on the Scriptures. Christianity without the Bible is a contradiction in terms. Preaching not anchored in the Scriptures is equally impossible. There is no true religious formation which is not based on the Gospel. The Bible is the letter which God himself wrote to humans in the thousands of years of their history. It is the long drawn-out sigh for Christ (Old Testament) and the account of his coming among us (New Testament).

When the temple of Jerusalem was burning, the Jews abandoned all its treasures to the flames but saved the Bible. Paul knew the Bible by heart, and Augustine said, "Ignorance of Scripture is ignorance of Christ."

The Bible is the word of God, the Word made flesh is the Eucharist. I put both of them on the altar and kneel down before them.

There's an awakening of interest in the Bible at the present time. Let us thank God for it; but we are still a long way from fully realizing the importance of the Bible in and to our lives.

I said earlier that prayer is like love. Words pour at first. Then we are more silent and can communicate in monosyllables. In difficulties a gesture is enough, a word, or nothing at all—love is enough. Thus the time comes when words are superfluous and meditation is difficult, almost impossible.

That is the time for the prayer of simplicity. The soul converses with God with a single loving glance, although this may often be accompanied by dryness and suffering.

In this period the so-called litanical prayer thrives; that is, repetitions of identical expressions, poor words, but very rich in content.

Hail Mary . . . Hail Mary . . . Jesus I love you. . . . Lord have mercy on me . . . My God and my all.

And it is strange how in these ejaculations, monotonous and simple, the soul finds itself at ease, almost cradled in God's arms. It is also a time for the rosary, lived and loved as one of the highest and most inspired prayers.

Often in my life as a European I have taken part in animated discussions on the pros and cons of the rosary. But in the end I was never fully satisfied. I was not in a fit condition to really understand this way of praying.

"It's a meditative prayer," some would say. Well, then, the young people are right to complain of the distractions which this useless repetition of ten Hail Marys bring to the meditation. Announce the mystery and leave me to my thoughts.

"No, it's a prayer of praise," others would say. "And one must think of what one is saying word by word."

But it's impossible! Who's capable of saying fifty Hail Marys distracted by the pictures of five mysteries without losing the thread?

I must confess that never in my life, although I have made the effort, have I succeeded in saying a single rosary without getting distracted.

It was in the desert that I came to realize that those who discuss the rosary—as I discussed it in that way—have not yet understood the soul of this prayer.

The rosary belongs to that type of prayer which precedes or accompanies the contemplative prayer of the spirit. Whether you meditate it or not, whether or not you get distracted, if you love the rosary deeply and can't let a day go by without saying it, you are already a person of prayer.

The rosary is like the echo of a wave breaking on the shore, God's shore: "Hail Mary . . . Hail Mary . . . Hail Mary . . ." It is like your mother's hand on your childhood cradle.

The rosary is a point of arrival, not of departure. For Bernadette the point of arrival came very soon, because she was destined to see Our Lady on this earth. But normally it is a prayer of spiritual maturity. If a young man doesn't like saying the rosary, and says he gets bored, don't force him. Reading a text from scripture is best for him, or maybe some more intellectual kind of prayer. But if you meet a child in the remote countryside, or a peaceful old man or a simple old woman who tells you they love the rosary without knowing why, rejoice and be glad, because the Holy Spirit prays in their hearts. The rosary is an incomprehensible prayer for the "commonsense" person, just as it is incomprehensible to repeat "I love you" a thousand times a day to a God one cannot see. But for the pure of heart it is understandable; the person rooted in the Kingdom and living the beatitudes understands the rosary.

The orthodox, who are highly contemplative, have developed a litanical prayer similar to our rosary; they call it "the Jesus prayer."

It is said by repeating slowly, again and again, with one's soul peacefully disposed, the Kyrie Eleison:

> Lord have mercy on me
> I am a sinful man
> Christ have mercy on me
> I am a sinful man

In this prayer they keep time with their breathing, or even their heartbeat.

As prayer becomes richer in content and uses fewer words, meditation grows difficult and distasteful. What before was a source of intellectual pleasure, now becomes dry and painful. One gets the impression of reaching a crossroad in the spiritual life. Sometimes one thinks he is going backward instead of making progress. The heavens have lost their bright colors, the soul feels "grey" in mood.

At this stage of spiritual life the person who has a good guide is fortunate, especially if one has the humility to let oneself be led.

It is not easy. We all think we know how to get along alone and only failure puts things in the right perspective.

What is this dryness in meditation which I am describing; this refusal to fix our thoughts on spiritual things? Clearly it may depend on some fault in ourselves. It may depend on some unhealthy attachment in our hearts, lack of vigilance, or the thorns in which we have let the good seed be choked. Difficulty in meditation is not always the sign of an advance of the soul towards God, or the progress to a higher type of prayer.

But it may, thank God, be a sign of that. How can one know the difference?

Again John of the Cross tells us.

There are three signs which indicate the movement from discursive to contemplative prayer:

1. We lack the desire to use the imagination.

2. The imagination and the senses no longer have the will to think about specific things. The things of the earth offer no consolation.

3. The soul wants to remain still, directed towards God alone. It desires inner peace, quiet and repose; it no longer feels the need to use the human faculties.

This third condition is good. If it is present in the soul it justifies the other two. If I have difficulty in meditating on God, if I no longer succeed in fixing my attention on one mystery or another in the life of Jesus, on one truth or another, but I am craving to remain alone and motionless and silent at the feet of God, empty of thought but in an act of love, . . . it means something great. It is one of the most beautiful secrets of the spiritual life.

CHAPTER 8

Contemplative Prayer

WE ARE NOW APPROACHING the essence of prayer. At this point we shall see the true penetration of God's revelation, the depth of God's mystery. We shall plumb the depths of our own being as Christians.

Jesus, on the night he was betrayed, said: "If you love me you will keep my commandments" (John 14:15).

Then he added: "Anybody who receives my commandments and keeps them will be one who loves me; and anybody who loves me will be loved by my Father and I shall love him and show myself to him" (John 14:21).

And he concluded: "If anyone loves me he will keep my word, and my Father will love him, and we shall come to him and make our home with him" (John 14:23).

God offers himself in three ways: his Spirit, his presence and his revelation of himself. And for these three offers he asks but one thing: "If a man loves me."

Those persons who offer God their love become "paradise on earth," the Trinity is a reality within them; they are an instrument of the Spirit and of God's will.

These three ways of God offering himself to us are

possible because of the death and resurrection of Christ, and are a reality because of him.

It is through prayer that we absorb this reality, for prayer establishes us in the deepest possible relationship with God. By our prayer we share the life of God.

The Trinity becomes a reality in us as the guest of the soul. Earth becomes heaven. Why go on searching for God beyond the stars when he is so close to us, within us. Heaven, this hidden place, is not some lofty vaulting construction, studded with stars. It is a land of intimate closeness, so near that we can speak to God, stay with him, worship him anywhere.

His Holy Spirit is in us.

He is the skilled craftsman who unites us with God. It is he who incorporates us in Christ Jesus, who teaches us what we must say to the Father. He creates a new spirit in us. He carries our prayer to the Most High and gives our feeble, childish yearnings value in the sight of God. How can I still say to myself, "Who will teach me to pray?" when I have a master like that at the center of my being? Why doubt the power of my prayer when, even if pathetic and stammering, its passage is sustained by the same Creator-Spirit?

No, I shall no longer try to pray by myself or rely on my own efforts, since in faith I have discovered that the Spirit of God is there in my heart.

But this is not enough. The promise of Jesus speaks of his presence, an activity of his Spirit, and of a revelation. "I shall make myself known to you."

Making themselves known to one another is the task of lovers; a task never finished, never complete. There always remains something mysterious to discover, an element of the unknown.

Think of God; in him everything is to be discovered. But in the case of God one thing must be made very clear. God is unknowable to humans directly. We can know him only through figures, symbols and signs. But they themselves are not God. Only God knows himself, and knowledge of him remains a mystery for us. But in his love God has decided to make himself known to us, to reveal himself to us. And that happens in a supernatural manner, in a language untranslatable on earth. A person who grasps this revelation can say nothing. He cannot repeat it.

Whoever wants to learn to pray must know this.

I have lost too much through knowing this truth too late. And yet it was clear in the Gospel.

I thought that in prayer everything depended on me and my efforts, on the books passing through my hands, and the beauty of the words which I was able to introduce into my conversations with God.

What is worse, I thought the knowledge of God I was acquiring through study and reasoning was the real and only one. I hadn't yet understood that it was only an image, a covering, an introduction to God's true and authentic revelation, which is supernatural and eternal.

God is unknowable, and only he can reveal himself to me through ways which are wholly his, unrepeatable in words and in concepts beyond our understanding.

So true prayer demands that we be more passive than active; it requires more silence than words, more adoration than study, more concentration than rushing about, more faith than reason. We must understand thoroughly that true prayer is a gift from heaven to earth, the Father to his child; from the Bridegroom to the bride, from him who has to one who has not, from Everything to nothing.

And the nearer this Everything comes to nothing, the more the unknowing becomes unlimited.

Of the person coming down from the mountain after having spoken at length with God, you ask: "Talk to us about Him." And he will repeat with Angela of Foligno, one of the great Italian mystics:

> Before God the soul is wrapped in his shadows and in them becomes acquainted with him more than I should ever have imagined it could; and with such splendor, such certainty and such depth that there is no human heart which can in any way understand or conceive such a thing.
>
> The soul can say absolutely nothing, because it has no words to express itself with. In fact, there is neither thought nor intelligence that can reach that far, so greatly does it surpass everything; the ways of God cannot be explained.
>
> When I again returned to myself, I knew for certain that those who feel God most deeply can say least about him. Precisely because they feel something of that infinite and unspeakable goodness, they can say less about it.

Of course it is pleasing to heaven that when you go to preach, you should understand. For if not, you would not be able to say anything at all about God. And so you would have to be silent! Then someone would come up to you and say: "Brother, speak to me a little about God," and you would not be able to say anything or think anything about God. His infinite goodness would overcome you.

But on the contrary the soul does not lose consciousness, the body does not lose any of its faculties. In fact, we are fully conscious.

But you would say to the people: "Go with God's blessing, because I can say nothing!" All the things that are said in the Scriptures and by the saints from the beginning of the world until now, seem to me to express hardly anything of the love of God; their words are like a speck of dust compared to the universe.

As it was for Angela of Foligno, so it is for all of us. We feel the knowledge of God becoming greater in us little by little as our love for him becomes greater. And of this knowledge we are unable to say anything. We know that it is a rich, mysterious, dark, personal knowledge of him; but we are not able to utter a syllable about what we know.

"I shall make myself known to you."

This revelation of himself which God makes to humans is the core, the fruit, the breath of contemplative prayer and it is a real sharing of eternal life. In John we find the definition of it: "Now this is everlasting life, that they may know thee, the only true God, and him whom thou hast sent, Jesus Christ" (John 17:3).

> O Lord, my heart is not proud
> nor haughty my eyes.
> I have not gone after things too great
> nor marvels beyond me.
>
> Truly I have set my soul
> In silence and peace.
> A weaned child on its mother's breast,
> even so is my soul. (Ps. 131)

This is the psalm of contemplative prayer. Human beings on the way to the roots of our being, toward our end, our creator, after having passed the first degrees of prayer, after having been purified by the suffering dryness of human pleasure and selfishness, find ourselves at the doorway of eternity. Our own strength can do nothing, meditation itself becomes impossible, and words, once so effortless, can only repeat some monosyllable of love and lament.

No image sums all this up so exactly as that of a child that has been weaned in its mother's arms. And it is still Jesus who tells us, "Unless you turn and become like little children, you will not enter into the Kingdom of Heaven" (Matthew 18:3). But by now the soul has made itself small and has understood that it must receive everything and that its only power is that of loving.

No, there is still the other power, that of knowing. But what use is that in such moments!

The anonymous medieval author of *The Cloud of Unknowing* says:

> But since all reasonable creatures, angels and men, have in them, each one by himself, one principal working power, the which is called a knowing power, and another principal working power, the which is called a loving power. Of the which two powers, to the first, the which is a knowing power, God who is the maker of them is evermore incomprehensible; but to the second, the which is the loving power, He is in every man diversely, all comprehensible to the full.

> One loving soul alone in itself, by virtue of love, may comprehend in itself Him who is sufficient to the full. And this is the endless marvelous miracle of love, the working of which shall never have end; for ever shall He do it, and never shall He cease for to do it.

It would seem strange at first sight. But nothing gives the sense of God's universality and his justice more than this truth. If God were attainable with the intelligence, how unjust it would be!

It would have made easy the task of the wise and the great of this world, and would have made knowledge of God all but impossible for the little ones, the poor, and the ignorant. But God himself has found the way to be equally accessible to everybody. His revelation comes in love, in that faculty which we can all share.

He loves equally queen and peasant, wise and ignorant.

"I bless you, Father, Lord of heaven and of earth, for hiding these things from the learned and the clever and revealing them to mere children."

But what becomes of concepts? They are not stifled. That would be contrary to the nature of our intelligence. The concepts are always there but are silent, and sleep like the apostles on the mountain.

That is what is known as infused contemplation or mystical knowledge. It feeds upon silence. It becomes negative in a new and absolute sense.

Hadewijch the Beguine says: "The single and naked truth abolished every kind of reasoning. It holds me in this emptiness and fits me for the simple life of eternity. All speech finishes here. He who has never understood the word of God would vainly explain what I have found without means, without a veil, above every reasoning."

Those who believe that they can speak of what is in the depths of their own soul betray their own inexperience. My God, what an adventure it is, not to understand any longer, nor be able to see. If earlier we possessed "something," love has now reduced us to nothing.

Yes, love has reduced us to nothing. It has taken from us all presumption of knowing or being. It has reduced us to true spiritual childhood.

> I have held my soul
> In peace and in silence
> As a child
> In its mother's arms.

This is the highest state of prayer: to be children in God's arms, silent, loving, rejoicing.

And if, through this desire of ours to say something, or do something, you feel that you must open your mouth, then do this: choose one word or a little phrase which well expresses your love for him; and then go on repeating it in peace, without trying to form thoughts, motionless in love before God who *is* love.

And with this word or this phrase transformed into an arrow of steel, a symbol of your love, beat again and again against God's thick cloud of unknowing.

Don't become distracted, whatever happens. Chase away even the good thoughts; they serve no purpose now.

The highest degree of contemplation one can attain in this life lies entirely in this darkness, this cloud of unknowing. With an impulse of love and a blind glance one is carried to the naked being of God himself and God alone.

A blind impulse of love, fixed on God himself, which presses secretly on the cloud of unknowing is nobler and more profitable for your soul, than any other spiritual exercise.

This is my wish, a synthesis of all the gifts which the desert has made me.

CHAPTER 9

Purification of the Spirit

THERE IS A SLOGAN known all over the world which runs, "If the money spent on slimming treatments and medicines for curing the after-effects of overeating in the well-to-do continents of Europe and America were put together, there would be enough money to give bread to the needy, undernourished peoples of Africa and Asia."

Which means that greed is one of the besetting sins of man, including intelligent, cultured, refined, and—all too often—religious people.

On this subject Jesus would say to us, "You have not managed to be faithful in little things. Who will entrust you with great things?" If we have demonstrated such greed at the table of the body, imagine how we would have behaved at the table of spiritual things, if we had felt ourselves attracted by it.

It is unnecessary to repeat it: we are sick, unbalanced, sensual, evil. And let there be no mistake: "we" means every one of us.

Jesus, in a true judgement of us summed up, "You who are all evil" (Matt. 7:11).

And he completed his judgement on the cross,

"Father forgive them, for they do not know what they are doing" (Luke 23:34).

Evil and insane. This is true of us in little things and in great: we have indigestion from overeating, yet let our neighbor starve, and this spreads over into our prayer and spiritual life.

But in order to hinder our spiritual indigestion God offers something radical: bare faith, simple hope, love without sentiment. Those who after their first steps in the spiritual life, throw themselves into the struggle of prayer and union with God, are astounded at the dryness of the road.

The more they advance, the more the darkness thickens around them. The more they go on, the more bitter and insipid everything becomes. They derive little comfort from the recollection of times past when God seemed to make their spiritual path easier.

Sometimes they are even tempted to shout, "But Lord, if you helped a little more, more people would follow you."

But God does not listen to such entreaty; rather, instead of consolation he sends boredom, and instead of light, darkness. Right there, halfway along our road, we don't know whether we are going backwards or forwards.

But only then the real battle begins and becomes serious. We are beginning to discover what we are worth: nothing, or little. At earlier stages we thought we were generous; we now discover that we are egoists. We thought, under the false light of religious aestheticism, that we knew how to pray; now we find that we no longer know how to say "Father." We were convinced that we were humble, charitable, obedient; now we find that pride has invaded our whole being, down to the deepest roots. Prayer, human relationships, working to spread the Gospel, all these seem thwarted.

But we must render our accounts, and these are very poor. With the exception of those privileged souls who understood right from the beginning what the problem really was, and who immediately set out upon the true, rough road of humility and spiritual childhood, the greater part of humankind is called upon to undergo a hard and painful experience.

This normally occurs around the age of forty: a great liturgical period in one's life, a Biblical period, a period of the noonday devil, the period of one's second youth, a crucial period for a person: "For forty years that generation repelled me, until I said: 'How unreliable these people who refuse to grasp my ways!'" (Psalm 95:10).

This is the time when God has decided to take those who until now have escaped behind a smokescreen of halfheartedness, and make them put their backs to the wall.

Disaster, boredom, depression, all these but especially the experience of sin make us discover what we really are. Poor, fragile, weak things; a mixture of pride and wickedness; inconstant, lazy, illogical.

There is no limit to this misery in humans. And God lets us drink the bitter cup to the dregs.

Even for those who in this situation do not sin because they are helped by grace, there opens up the vision of things as they really are: God, human being, sin.

The soul becomes aware that it is walking on a tightrope. And beneath it can see the hell which it has merited a hundred times, and a hundred times escaped, by God's mercy.

There is no sin which it has not committed, or which it does not feel truly capable of committing. But this is not enough.

In the depths lodges the most crucial fault, greater than any other even though it is hidden. It rarely, or perhaps never, breaks out in single concrete actions pushing towards the surface of the world. But from the depths, from the inmost layers of our being, it soaks in a poison which causes extreme damage. It is a fault which appears more in general attitudes than in individual actions, but it is this, rather than the actions themselves, which determine the real quality of the human heart. Because it is hidden, or rather camouflaged, we can barely catch sight of it, and often only after a long time; but it is alive enough in our consciousness to be able to contaminate us and it weighs us down considerably more than the things which we habitually confess. These attitudes envelop our whole life like an atmosphere and are present, as it were, in every action or omission. They are hidden and general sins we cannot rid ourselves of: laziness and cowardice, a falsehood and vanity, from which not even our prayer can be entirely free. They burden our whole existence and damage it. The time for playing games at spirituality, for "Let's pretend," is over. One has got as far as knowing one's ignorance. One stands on the edge of the abyss which separates the creature from the Creator.

There one can live but on alms, and on the grace that can be neither known nor grasped.

Every means has proved powerless, every path too short. God's impenetrable night wraps round us. Terrible loneliness accompanies us, but this is necessary and inevitable.

Every word of consolation seems like a lie. One believes one has been abandoned by God.

In this deeply painful state, prayer becomes true and strong even though it may be as dry as dust.

The soul speaks to its God out of its poverty and pain; still more out of its impotence and abjection.

Words become even fewer and barer. One is reduced to silence, but this is a step forward in prayer! It is limitless, whereas every word has a limit. And spiritual greed?

Oh, that's always there! It hides under the ashes, but it is less violent, more prudent.

God now again intervenes with his consolation, since it would be impossible to live in that state of abandonment. He returns to encourage the soul with the touch of his gentleness. The soul accepts that touch with gratitude. But it has become so timid through the blows it has received that it dare not ask anything more.

Deep down the soul has understood that it must let itself be carried, that it must abandon itself to its Savior, that alone it can do nothing, that God can do every-thing.

And if it remains still and motionless, as though bound in the faithfulness of God, it will quickly realize that things have changed, and that its progress, though still painful, is in the right direction.

It is the direction of love! This realization will come like light after darkness, the midday sun after the dawn.

What matters is to let God get on with it.

Chapter 10

Contemplation in the Streets

At this point, my friend, I am sure there is a question in your mind, accompanied by a slight smile.

"Well, then! Is there no value in action, duty to our fellow humans, plunging oneself like leaven into this secular city? Must we all go into the desert? Is that possible? The desert is far away, I shall never be able . . ."

I know that's what you were thinking, and I must explain myself quite clearly, because something really crucial is at stake.

Charles de Foucauld said one day: "If the contemplative life were possible only behind convent walls or in the silence of the desert we should, in fairness, give a little convent to every mother of a family, and a track of desert to every person working hard in a bustling city to earn his living."

The vision of the reality in which the majority of poor men and women live determined the central crisis of his life; the crisis which was to carry him far from his first understanding of the religious life.

As you may know, Charles de Foucauld was a Trappist, and had chosen the poorest Trappist monastery in existence, that of Akbès in Syria. One day his superior sent him to watch by the corpse of a Christian Arab who had died in a poor house.

When Brother Charles was in the dead man's hovel he saw real poverty around him: hungry children and a weak, defenseless widow without assurance of the next day's bread. It was this spiritual crisis which was to make him leave La Trappe and go in search of a religious life very different from the earlier one.

"We, who have chosen the imitation of Jesus and Jesus Crucified, are very far from the trials, the pains, the insecurity and the poverty to which these people are subjected.

"I no longer want a monastery which is too secure. I want a small monastery, like the house of a poor workman who is not sure if tomorrow he will find work and bread, who with all his being shares the suffering of the world."

"Oh, Jesus, a monastery like your house at Nazareth, in which to live hidden as you did when you came among us."

When he came out of La Trappe Foucauld founded his first fraternity at Beni-Abbès in the Sahara; later he built his hermitage at Tamanrasset where he died, murdered by the Tuareg.

The fraternity was to resemble the house of Nazareth, a house just like one of the many houses one sees along the many streets of the world.

Had he renounced contemplation then? Had his fervid spirit of prayer weakened? No, he had taken a step

Charles de Foucauld

forward. He had decided to live the contemplative life along the streets, in a situation similar to that of any ordinary man.

That step is much harder!

It is a step that God wants humankind to make.

The life of Charles de Foucauld opens up a new understanding of the spiritual life in which many will force themselves to make the fusion between contemplation and action—really living and obeying the first commandment of the Lord, "Love God above all things and your neighbour as yourself."

"Contemplation in the streets." This is tomorrow's task not only for the Little Brothers, but for all the poor.

Let us begin to analyze this element of "desert" which must be present, especially today, in the carrying out of such a demanding program.

When one speaks of the soul's desert, and says that the desert must be present in your life, you must not think only of the Sahara or the desert of Judea, or into the High Valley of the Nile.

Certainly it is not everyone who can have the advantage of being able to carry out in practice this detachment from daily life. The Lord conducted me into the real desert because I was so thick-skinned. For *me,* it was necessary. But all that sand was not enough to erase the dirt from my soul, even the fire was not enough to remove the rust from Ezekiel's pot.

But the same way is not for everybody. And if you cannot go into the desert, you must nonetheless "make some desert" in you life. Every now and then leaving men and looking for solitude to restore, in prolonged silence and prayer, the stuff of your soul. This is the meaning of "desert" in your spiritual life.

One hour a day, one day a month, eight days a year, for longer if necessary, you must leave everything and everybody and retire, alone with God. If you don't look for this solitude, if you don't love it, you won't achieve real contemplative prayer. If you are able to do so but nevertheless do not withdraw in order to enjoy intimacy with God, the fundamental element of the relationship with the All-Powerful is lacking: love. And without love no revelation is possible.

But the desert is not the final stopping place. It is a stage on the journey. Because, as I told you, our vocation is contemplation in the streets.

For me, this is quite costly. The desire to continue living here in the Sahara forever is so strong that I am already suffering in anticipation of the order that will certainly come from my superiors: "Brother Carlo, leave for Marseilles, leave for Morocco, leave for Venezuela, leave for Detroit.

"You must go back among people, mix with them, live your intimacy with God in the noise of their cities. It will be difficult but you must do it. And for this the grace of God will not fail you.

"Every morning, after Mass and meditation, you will make your way to work in a store or shipyard. And when you get back in the evening, tired, like all poor men forced to earn their living, you will enter the little chapel of the brotherhood and remain for a long time in adoration; bringing to your prayer all that world of suffering, of darkness, and often of sin, in the midst of which you have lived for eight hours taking your share of pain and toil."

Contemplation in the streets. A good phrase, but very demanding.

Certainly it would be easier and more pleasant to stay here in the desert. But God doesn't seem to want that.

The voice of the Church makes itself heard more and more. It points out to Christians the reality of the Mystical Body and the People of God. It calls us to the life of love. It invites everybody to a life of action which, couched in contemplation, is a witness and presence among others.

Convent walls are becoming thinner and the ceilings ever lower. The laity are becoming conscious of their mission and are searching for a genuine spirituality. It is truly the dawn of a new world to which it would not seem unworthy to give as an aim "contemplation in the streets" and to offer the means of achieving it.

But there is another basic element of the contemplative life, above all as it is lived in the world: poverty.

Poverty is not a question of having or not having money. Poverty is not material. It is a beatitude. "Blessed are the poor in spirit." It is a way of being, thinking and loving. It is a gift of the Spirit. Poverty is detachment, and freedom and, above all, truth.

Go into almost any middle-class home, even a Christian one, and you will see the lack of this beatitude of poverty. The furniture, the drapes, the whole atmosphere are stereotyped, determined by fashion and luxury, not by necessity and truth.

This lack of liberty, or rather this slavery to fashion, is one of the idols which attracts a great number of Christians. How much money is sacrificed upon its altar!—without taking into account that so much good could otherwise be done with it. Being poor in spirit means, above all, being unrestrained by what is called fashion; it means freedom.

I don't buy a blanket because it is fashion. I buy it because I need it. Without a blanket my child shivers in bed. Bread, a blanket, a table, fire, are things necessary in themselves. To use them is to carry out God's plan. "All the rest comes from the evil one," to paraphrase an expression of Jesus' about truth. And this "rest" is fashion, habit, luxury, over-indulgence, greed—slavery to the world.

One seeks not what is true, but what is pleasing to others. We seem to need this mask. We seem incapable of living without it.

Things get really serious when "styles" come into the picture and prices become astronomical. "This is a Louis XIV—this is genuine crystal—this is etc., etc."

It is more serious still when "styles" enter the homes of churchmen, called by God to preach the Gospel to the poor.

There was a period during which churchly opulence might possibly have been justified.

From the Renaissance to the eighteenth century, the triumphant posture of the Church and the need felt by the masses to give worthy honor to God and the things of God, were expressed with extraordinary luxury and pomp.

The poor then were not scandalized; indeed they seemed pleased with all that glitter and magnificence.

Even more recently I remember my mother who, although poor, spoke with "Christian" pride and satisfaction of the beauty of the bishop's house, and the length of the prelate's car parked under the window.

But things have changed. If that same bishop today knew of, or rather heard, the curses hurled at his long, elegant car, he would quickly change it for an economy model or better still, he'd use a bicycle.

We speak increasingly of the Church of the Poor, and I don't think it's a merely rhetorical phrase.

It's necessary, however, to understand the meaning of the words. When one speaks of poverty in the Church one must not identify it with the beatitude of poverty. This, the beatitude, is an interior virtue, and I cannot, and must not judge my brother by it. Even the wealthy person, or the pontiff covered with a golden cope, can and must possess the beatitude of poverty. Nobody can judge another in this respect.

But when one speaks of poverty in the Church, one means social poverty, care for the poor, help for the poor, preaching the Gospel to the poor.

When one speaks of poverty in the Church, one means the kind of life Christians live, and this it is which scandalizes the poor, as Paul was scandalized by the behavior of the Christians of Corinth.

> The point is, when you hold these meetings, it is not the Lord's Supper that you are eating, since when the time comes to eat, everyone is in such a hurry to start his own supper that one person goes hungry while another is getting drunk. Surely you have homes for eating and drinking in? Surely you have enough respect for the community of God not to make poor people embarrassed? (1 Cor. 11:20-22)

And don't we perhaps put the poor man to shame when we pass by with our power and riches while he cannot afford to pay the rent? How can we preach the Gospel to him, while enjoying economic security when he doesn't know whether tomorrow he will have work and bread?

But poverty as a beatitude is not only truth, freedom and justice. It is and always will be love, and its limits become infinite, as infinite as the love of God.

Poverty is love for the poor Jesus, and voluntary self-denial. Jesus could have been rich. He did not have to live the kind of life he lived. No, he wanted to be poor in order to share the restrictions of real poverty, to put up with the lack of comfort, to suffer in his body the hard reality which weighs down the man searching for bread, to experience the abiding instability of one who possesses nothing.

This authentic poverty, borne for the sake of love, is the true beatitude of which the Gospel speaks.

It is easy to speak of spiritual poverty, to fill one's mouth with pious words, and yet not lack anything, not really feel the pinch, have a secure house, a well-stocked larder and the security of a bank account.

Let us not deceive ourselves and let us not dilute the most precious things Jesus said.

Poverty is poverty and always will be poverty; and it is not enough to make a vow of poverty in order to be "poor in spirit."

Today the poor are a real cause for scandal; to be rid of this scandal it would be better to spend less time arguing about the nature of chastity and put more emphasis on this beatitude which is in danger of being forgotten by those who are trying to "live as Christians." If it is true, as it is, that the perfection of the law is love, then it must fully control my desire for possessions and riches. Otherwise I shall not know what the beatitude really means.

If I love, if I really love, how can I tolerate the fact that a third of humanity is menaced with starvation while I enjoy the security of economic stability? If I act in that way I shall perhaps be a good Christian, but I shall certainly not be a saint; and today there are far too many good Christians when the world needs saints. We must learn to accept instability, put ourselves every now and then in the condition of having to say, "Give us this day our daily bread," with real anxiety because the larder is empty; have the courage, for love of God and one's neighbor, to give until it hurts and, above all, keep open in the wall of the soul the great window of living faith in the Providence of an all-powerful God.

I know that what I have said about poverty is challenging, and I also know that when in the world I did not really put it into practice. It is I who have lived for years behind the mask of "pleasing others"; it is I who have spent money, and not only my own, on things which are "not real."

And yet, in spite of this, I cannot remain silent; and to my friends I must say: beware of the temptation of riches. It is much more serious than it may appear today to well-intentioned Christians, and it sows destruction primarily because we underestimate its danger.

Riches are a slow poison, which strikes almost imperceptibly, paralyzing the soul at the moment when it seems healthiest. They are thorns which grow with the grain and suffocate it right at the moment when the corn is beginning to shoot up. What a number of men and women, religious people, let themselves get caught up in their later lives by the spirit of middle-class tastes.

Now that solitude and prayer have helped me to see things more clearly, I understand why contemplation and poverty are inseparable. It is impossible to have a deep relationship with Jesus in Bethlehem, with Jesus in exile, with Jesus the workman of Nazareth, with Jesus the apostle who has nowhere to lay his head, with the cruci-fied Jesus, without having achieved within ourselves that detachment from things, proclaimed with such authority and lived by him.

One will not reach this high state of poverty at once. Indeed, life itself will not be long enough to achieve it fully. But we must think about it, reflect and, above all, pray.

Jesus, God of the impossible, will help us. He will work, if need be, the miracle of making the parable of the camel pass though the narrow rusty eye of our poor sick soul.

Chapter 11

Sectarianism

THIS EVENING ABDARAMAN is accompanying me to the hermitage for adoration. We walk the two hundred yards together, hand in hand and chatting.

Abdaraman is a Muslim boy of perhaps eight years old. I say "perhaps" because no Registry of Births exists among his people; a child's birth is simply not recorded. So few people know their exact age.

Abdaraman does not go to school, even though there is one beyond the river, attended by the Europeans and some "Mosabites," the sons of local tradesmen. He doesn't go to school because his father Aleck won't let him go.

"Aleck," I asked him, "why don't you send your sons to school?" Aleck looked at me deeply. "Brother Carlo, I don't send my sons to school because they become bad. Look at the boys who go to school. They don't pray, they no longer obey, and they care about nothing but the way they dress."

Abdaraman is quite naked. He looks like a beautiful dark-grey statue, the result of infinite crossings between black Africans brought here as slaves, and white Africans from Northern tribes: Arabs, Berbers, and Tuareg.

Abdaraman, like all the sons of Ishmael, is circumcised and of the strict observance. His father Aleck is a good man, with strong faith and many sons. When the month of Ramadan comes around he fasts from dawn to dusk though continuing to work in his field along the banks of the river at Tamanrasset. Aleck is very devout and every year he remembers the sacrifice of Abraham by the killing of a sheep; then he buys a pale cotton dress for each of his little ones. His faith in God is absolute, and, poor as he is, he does not steal, but lives from his work. This consists in digging a canal, called a *seghia,* for months at a time in the sands of the river bank, and for the other months cultivating his little field, which needs water at least three times a week.

Once a detachment of the Foreign Legion arrived and pitched camp along the *seghia* which carries water to Aleck's corn. Soon the water ran short and Aleck's corn began to wither.

"Aleck," I said to him, "if it goes on like this your corn will dry up. Go and tell the captain the *seghia* is yours, and to pitch his camp elsewhere."

Aleck answered, "Allah is great and will provide for my children." And he let the corn die while the legionnaires washed their vehicles and threw water at one another in fun.

Abdaraman is accompanying me this evening to the hermitage. The sun has set and the air has freshened. It's good to walk. We always have many things to talk about because we are really fond of one another. Every morn-

ing I find him outside my cell waiting for me to finish my meditation. Often we have tea together and he tells me how much he likes the bread I make. Abdaraman is always hungry. But he never asks me for anything; it's always I who have to guess that he wants food.

This evening he is serious, and answers my questions with difficulty. I realize that he has something important to say to me and hesitates to do so.

But I know it won't be long before he speaks, because there are no secrets between him and me.

"What's the matter, Abdaraman?"

Silence.

"Are you hungry?"

Silence.

"Did Daddy spank you?"

Silence.

"Has your bird escaped from its cage?"

Silence.

"Speak to me, Abdaraman. You know I am your friend."

Abdaraman bursts into tears, his naked body shaking. Tears stream down his face and then continue down onto his chest and abdomen.

Now it's my turn to be silent. I must await the stilling of the storm. I squeeze his hands harder as a sign of affection.

"Well, then, Abdaraman, what's making you cry?"

"Brother Carlo, I am crying because you don't become a Muslim!"

"Oh," I exclaim, "and why should I become a Muslim? Abdaraman, I am a Christian, and believe in Jesus. I believe in the God who created heaven and earth, just as you do, and our prayers go to the same heaven, because there's only one God. It is he who has created us, who feeds us and loves us. If you do your duty, don't rob, don't kill, don't tell lies, and follow the voice of your conscience, then you'll go to heaven, and it'll be the same heaven as mine, if I too have done what God commanded me. Don't cry any more."

"No, no," Abdaraman cries. "If you don't become a Muslim you'll go to hell like all Christians!"

"Oh, what a thought, Abdaraman! Who told you I would go to hell if I didn't become a Muslim?"

"A man in the village told me that all Christians go to hell. And I don't want you to go to hell."

We have almost reached the hermitage, and Abdaraman stops. He has never come any further than this. He has always stopped ten steps away from that building, and he would not enter for all the gold in the world, as though inside there were some mysterious deviltry forbidden to little Muslims. His love for me, and it is great, has always been injured by this wall which divides us and which this evening is taking on such an absolutely terrible name—hell.

I tell him, "No, Abdaraman. God is good and will save both of us. He will save your father, too, and we shall all go to heaven. Don't believe that just because I am a Christian I shall go to hell, as I don't believe you'll go there just because you're a Muslim. God is so good! Perhaps you didn't understand really what the man meant. Perhaps he said that bad Christians go to hell. Cheer up! Go home and say your prayers while I say mine. And before you finish, say this to God and I'll say it too: 'Lord, let all men be saved!' Go on . . ." And sadly I entered the hermitage, this little mud building, constructed by the same Charles de Foucauld who wanted to be called the Little Brother of all men and who was murdered, through ignorance and fanaticism, by sons of the same tribe as Aleck and Abdaraman.

But this evening it is difficult for me to pray. What a tumult of thoughts my little friend has aroused in me!

Poor little Abdaraman! You, too, are a victim of fanaticism, the stormy zeal of religious people, the so-called "men of God," who would send half the human race to hell, just because they are not "one of us." How can the thread of love which links me to a brother be broken by an alleged purity of faith, or that religion, instead of being a bridge of union, should become a trench of death, or at least of unconfessed hate? We're best off without it, this religion which divided us. Best to fumble around in the dark, than to possess a light like that!

After an hour's effort to face my poor soul with the silence of the Eucharist, I realized that tears were staining my white robe. I was the one to weep now.

While examining my conscience in order to cleanse *my* soul, not Abdaraman's, from sectarianism, a scene from my childhood rose again to my mind. I was eight years old then, the same age as Abdaraman. I lived in a village in the shade of an ancient church tower. The townspeople were not very religious, but they were excessively narrow-minded in their "purity of faith."

One day a man came to sell books, going from house to house. I didn't understand much then, but it was the first time I understood the word Bible.

An unusual commotion seized the village. First the women, then everybody. Some out of zeal, some out of human respect. The excitement quickly reached the children.

The hysterical cry of a woman shouting from a window: "Rascal! You rascal! We don't need your religion. Go away!"

The man was walking in the middle of the street. His books were in a big, heavy bag.

A woman from behind him threw a book she had bought a few minutes before. Without turning around, the man bent down to pick it up. A stone from a boy hit him in the back. The man quickened his pace, followed at some distance by the boys, each carrying a stone. I was among them. That evening at May Devotions the parish priest praised us for defending the parish citadel.

At a distance of forty years, and particularly this evening, that event acquired a new meaning for me.

I had never confessed to throwing a stone at an undefended man, out of religious zeal at that. The episode is recorded in a world which used to accept things of that kind, without seeing all their heinousness.

Nearly half a century later things have changed. There is something new in the air. A breath from the Spirit is animating the whole universe. An old world is dying, and a new one is being born. New concerns, new needs, new forces. We are at the dawn of an epoch marked by a great desire, at least, for love and peace among peoples and nations. Truth and charity are again striving to meet one another; respect for the individual is increasingly championed among all peoples.

An ecumenical spirit is loosening the most complicated knots, and the desire to know one another is far greater than the temptation to remain closed in the old citadel of our presumed truth.

Humanity, perhaps for the first time, is going into the field undefended, hopeful of fruitful encounters, of making friends of strangers.

Abdaraman, my dear little Abdaraman, have no fear: we shall love one another again, and we shall meet one another—and not only in heaven.

Chapter 12

Nazareth

Charles de Foucauld, born in Strasbourg September 15, 1858, was a nobleman. In his veins ran the blood of proud people accustomed to giving commands. He himself had attended the military academy of Saint Cyr, become an officer in the French army, and at the age of twenty-five had embarked on what was then a most dangerous undertaking—the exploration of Morocco.

Yet this man, soldier, adventurer—and apostate since his schooldays at Nancy—suddenly, in 1886, fell in love with Christ with the strength of a Saint Francis.

Very rarely does one find a man more passionately dedicated to discovering the details of the life of Jesus. He searched in the Gospels for clues to Jesus' personality, character, and life, so that he might imitate the Lord's attitude, gestures, and innermost intentions; and in his loving search for faithful and living material for imitation, Charles de Foucauld was above all impressed by the fact that Jesus was poor and a workman. Astonishing! The Son of God—who, more than anyone else, was free to choose what he would—chose not only a mother and a people, but also a social position. And he wanted to be a wage earner.

That Jesus had *voluntarily* lost himself in an obscure Middle Eastern village; annihilated himself in the daily monotony of thirty years' rough, miserable work; separated himself from the society that "counts"; and died in total anonymity—all this confused the noble convert. (We must realize that the words "Laborer," "worker," and "wage earner" have a quite different ring in the ears of a nobleman than they have in the average person's. Therefore it seemed to Charles de Foucauld that choosing to become a worker meant abasement, annihilation of oneself.) Why hadn't Jesus become a scribe, he wondered? Why hadn't he wished to be born into one of those families destined for command, responsibility, social and political influence?

Not too long after de Foucauld began the passionate search for the intentions which had guided the Divine Master in the choice of his life, his whole life, he made the discovery that was to remain, basically, the ascetical guide of the life of this great Moroccan explorer and Saharan mystic: "Jesus has so diligently searched for the lowest place that it would be very difficult for anyone to tear it from him."

Nazareth was the lowest place: the place of the poor, the unknown, of those who didn't count, of the mass of workers, of men subjected to work's grim demands just for a scrap of bread.

But there is more. Jesus is the "Holy One of God." But the Holy One of God realized his sanctity not in an extraordinary life, but one impregnated with ordinary things: work, family and social life, obscure human activities, simple things shared by all men and women.

The perfection of God is cast in a material which people almost despise, which they don't consider worth searching for because of its simplicity, its lack of interest, because it is common to everyone.

Once he had discovered the spiritual reality of Nazareth, Charles de Foucauld tried to imitate it as faithfully as possible.

He tried to found a community in a small home like the one at Nazareth; he tried to lose himself in the silence of an unknown village; he imitated Jesus by working manually, and he wanted his Little Brothers to be always searching for the last place, there where the poor are, where the climate is roughest, the wages the most meager, the toil hardest. Nazareth symbolized all this, and more.

The imitation of Nazareth is no small thing. When I think that a door, a wooden partition, was all that divided a holy family like that of Jesus' from that of a neighbor, I am convinced of the immense interior richness of the Gospel message. The same actions, if carried out under God's light, radically transformed the life of man, family and society.

Joy or sadness, war or peace, love or hate, purity or impurity, charity or greed, all are tremendous realities which are the hinges of a man's interior life. Everyday things, relationships with our fellow men and women, daily work, love of our family—all these may breed saints.

Jesus at Nazareth taught us to live every hour of the day as saints. Every hour of the day is useful and may lead to divine inspiration, the will of the Father, the prayer of contemplation—holiness. Every hour of the day is holy. What matters is to live it as Jesus taught us.

And for this one does not have to shut oneself in a monastery or fix strange and inhumane regimes for one's life. It is enough to accept the realities of life. Work is one of these realities; motherhood, the rearing of children, family life with all its obligations are others.

These realities must be sanctified; we must not think that a person is holy just because he has made vows. One with this outlook thinks of the hour of spiritual reading or prayer as the only time for the spiritual life and ignores the longer time dedicated to work and everyday living. The result is at best an anemic and unreliable religious personality.

The whole person must be transformed by the Gospel message. Nothing one does can be indifferent. All one's actions must be determined by the Gospel.

Nazareth is the life of a person, of a family, fully engaged in human activity.

Few have summed up the sanctity of common things so well as did Gandhi in his writings:

> If when we plunge our hand
>   into a bowl of water,
> Or stir up the fire with the bellows
> Or tabulate interminable columns of figures
>   on our book-keeping table,

> Or, burnt by the sun, we are plunged in
>   the mud of the rice-field,
> Or standing by the smelter's furnace
> We do not fulfill the same religious life
>   as if in prayer in a monastery,
>   the world will never be saved.

But there's another aspect of Nazareth which is important above all for those who think it is impossible to carry out the Gospel message without tools, means or money.

Jesus was himself the carrier of the message; he was at the same time the Supreme Intelligence, capable of devising the best way of making himself understood, and of carrying out the divine plans.

Well, what did he do? He did not open hospitals or found orphanages. He became flesh, lived among people and he embodied the Gospel message in its entirety, *Coepit facere.* He began to act.

He *lived* his message before he *spoke* of it. He preached it by his life before explaining it in words. This was Jesus' method and we too easily forget it.

In many cases catechesis is reduced to words rather than to "life," to discussions rather than to the pursuit of Christian living.

And here, perhaps, is the reason for the poor results, and still more, the reason for so much of the apathy and indifference among Christians today. Teaching is ineffective because it is not life-centered; there is no life because there is no example; there is no example because empty words have taken the place of faith and charity.

"I want to preach the Gospel with my life," Charles de Foucauld often said. He was convinced that the most effective method of preaching the Gospel was to live it. Especially today, people no longer want to listen to sermons. They want to see the Gospel in action.

Nazareth is the long period of separation, prayer and sacrifice. It is a time of silence, of intimate life with God; the time of long solitude, purification, understanding men, and knowing the value of detachment: the things that matter to a Christian.

From Nazareth we will learn how to live the Gospel, to be apostles. What does it mean to be an apostle?

The word is one of the most misunderstood today. It is a term used both correctly and incorrectly. Everybody has become an apostle, and even moving a chair counts as apostolic activity.

Perhaps we have gotten into the habit of using big words to enhance parochial or diocesan life; but things don't change and words remain words.

All I should like to say on the subject is that having meditated for a long time on Nazareth, I have learned from the depths of this mystery a deeper appreciation of the life of the layman and the life of the priest, of the apostolate of the laity and the apostolate of the priest.

My generation has lived through an extraordinary and in many ways chaotic period and many things must be justified either by reason of our childish incompetence and lack of preparation, or attributed to special historical circumstances.

After all, when a house is on fire, even a woman may do the fireman's job, and a layman gives orders to a bishop.

But normally these things should not be. It is not for the layman to undertake the curate's duties, nor for the priest to be the parish bookkeeper. As for me, in the middle of the desert, as the termites eat up the books in my cell, it is enough to think of Nazareth. To me the greatest inspiration for the spirituality of the laity is in the life of Jesus, Mary, and Joseph.

The spirituality of the laity shouldn't be a copy, good or bad, of that of priests, but something else: authentic and genuine in its own right, true before God and humans. The activity of a priest is one thing, the activity of a politician another; the activity of a pastor is one thing, that of a worker or the parent of a family another.

If it is true that by spirituality we mean the way of thinking, living and sanctifying the acts of our lives, then the way in which a priest lives and sanctifies the acts of his life is something profoundly different from the way in which a worker, a married person or a civil servant does.

Laypersons are not to be quasi-priests. They must sanctify their work, their marriage, their varied relationships as laypersons.

Saint Peter, in his first epistle (2:4) says to the laity: "You, too, must be a holy priesthood to offer up the

spiritual sacrifice which Jesus Christ has made acceptable to God, living stones making a spiritual house."

There is no question then that a real and authentic
priesthood exists for baptized Christians. It is very different, naturally, from the priesthood conferred by the
sacrament of Holy Orders, but it is a real priesthood
which the layperson must live and develop in its own
right.

This is extremely important, and the layperson who
does not respond to it has either betrayed or failed to
understand his or her vocation.

The worker is a priest in his or her work; the father
of a family is a priest for his wife and children; the head
of a community is a priest before its members; the peasant is a priest for his farm, animals, fields and flowers.

The royal priesthood of which Peter spoke and the
meaning of the "offering of spiritual sacrifices which
Jesus Christ has made acceptable to God" have been
emphasized too little. This has created the dryness appar-
ent in so much discussion on the apostolate of the laity,
and, what is more, of the position of the layperson in the
Church.

How can we speak of the spirituality of the laity if we
omit this fundamental prerogative of the priest of created things, voice of nature, consecrator of the goods of
the earth, saint of the earthly city?

If this is not expounded the laypersons who wished
to become "good" will end up by copying the parish
priest, whom they feel to be spiritually ahead of them,

and they will become half lay and half priest. This may be to the edification of the good parishioners, but perhaps of no influence on those outside, especially the "lapsed."

These latter—rightly—cannot bear the scent of religious hybrids and they continue to think that Christianity has no answer to the world's problems.

There is still a long way to go, but some progress has been made.

Priests and laity have begun to realize their respective roles in the Church.

That's what I hope for, because I would like those who enter this arena of apostolic activity today to avoid the false assumptions of my time, whereby priests were dragged in as canvassers, and the laity expected to give advice to the bishops on the Church government.

CHAPTER 13

The Last Place

I BECAME A LITTLE Brother of Jesus because God called me. I never doubted the call. Equally, if God hadn't called me I couldn't have survived for long!

Sleeping in the open, living in rough climates, associating with really poor tribes and putting up with the stench: all this is small compared with the revolution in one's personality, the breaking off with the past, the living among civilizations and peoples so different from one's own.

As you know, the Little Brother may not have a life apart. He must choose a village, a slum, a nomadic town, settle in it and live as all the others live, especially as the poorest live.

This is quite contrary to the behavior of Europeans who had previously come here. The European arrived as a soldier, missionary, technician or official, built himself a European house and lived as a European among the natives. His standard of living was not the local one, but that of his country of origin.

His task was to spread the Gospel, educate, help, organize, support; but always in the European way, with European culture, methods and aims. These men preached their faith by what they gave.

And that's no small thing! Miracles of love and heroism were written in the earth of Africa and Asia: churches, hospitals, dispensaries, schools, social institutions were created in order to cure disease, avert death and hasten the progress of people in underdeveloped countries.

It was the great missionary moment of the Church; it coincided with the growth of colonization and empire-building.

It represented the infiltration of the white race into the colored ones, the movement of the rich towards the poor, Christians towards "pagan." Things didn't always go smoothly; a missionary wasn't always synonymous with a man of God, nor an official with generosity and justice.

It's a long story. If we went on with it we should end by bringing the past to trial, and our only interest is the way in which in a few years everything has begun to change.

The African churches are becoming aware of their own identity and no longer wish to be copies of the English, the Italian or the Dutch churches. Not only do colored people no longer tolerate colonialism; through reaction, they are closing their hearts to the white man, they no longer have the trust they once had, and often they despise or hate everything which comes from the "master race" of former times.

As is natural in such cases, this reaction can be excessive and result in injustice and intolerance if one sees only what was bad in the past.

It is more true than ever that we must review past positions, reconsider all the attitudes.

In this light, and in view of the new attitudes to mission work in the Church today, the work of Charles de Foucauld can be seen as prophetic.

This man of God, never truly aware of the problems but driven on by the strength and light of the Spirit, went to Africa in the period of full colonization. At that time, there was not the slightest indication of the way in which events would turn in Africa. Caring only about carrying the Gospel to the Berbers or the Tuareg, he understood what others did not, and worked as though the process of decolonization had already begun.

He did not arrive with gifts, hospitals, dispensaries, schools and money.

He arrived alone, defenseless, poor. He had understood that the power of the European, even if expressed in hospitals and schools, had hardly anything to say to the African on the spiritual level and was no longer the witness it had once been.

He understood that the native, however poor and ill-educated, was no longer willing to accept as from on high a message which seemed entirely bound to a particular people and a particular civilization.

Someone had to show a new way; in a sense it was not a new way, for it was there in the Gospel. But it had to be lived with a new purity and strength: It is the way of poverty, sacrifice, humility, and silent witness. It is arguable that this is the way not only for poor countries; people everywhere are afraid of power. The powerful, rich, dominating Church of today makes people afraid.

The human eye, terrorized by the possibility it sees in science, rests joyfully upon what is little, undefended, weak. People are even afraid of an orator who shouts too loudly.

Here is the secret of the wide acceptance of Charles de Foucauld. He arrived, undefended, among savage tribesmen like the Tuareg. He came to the Arab world dressed as an Arab. He lived among those who were the servants of the Europeans as though they were his masters. He built his hermitages, not on Roman or Gothic lines, but on the simplicity and poverty of the Saharan mosques.

Being poor, dressing like "them," accepting their language and customs, he immediately knocked down the barriers and lived in dialogue with them. Real dialogue: between equals.

I shall never forget a scene which, in its simplicity, expresses concretely the degree of love in this new "going towards them who do not yet know Christ."

I was traveling by camel along the track between Geriville and El Abiod, heading for a desert area to spend some days in solitude.

At a certain point along the track I came to a work detail. About fifty natives, under the direction of a minor official of the Engineer Corps, were toiling to repair the road, ruined by the winter rain.

No machines, no technology under the Saharan sun; only the toil of wielding the shovel and pick all day in

the heat and the dust. I passed up the line of workmen scattered on the track, replying to their greetings and offering the liters of water in my *gherba* for their thirst.

At a certain point, among the mouths approaching the *gherba* to drink, I saw a smile break out which I shall never forget.

Poor, ragged, sweating, dirty: it was Brother Paul, a Little Brother who had chosen that detail in which to live out his Calvary, to be a kind of leaven there.

Nobody would have detected the European underneath those clothes, that beard and that turban, yellow from the dust and the sun.

I knew Brother Paul well, because we had been novices together.

A Parisian engineer, he had been working on the Reganna atomic bomb when he heard the Lord's call.

He left everything, and became a Little Brother. Now he was there. Nobody knew he was an engineer. He was a poor man like the others.

I remember his mother when she came to the novitiate on the occasion of him making his vows.

"Brother Carlo," she had said, "help me understand my son's vocation! I have made him an engineer; you have made him a manual laborer. Why? You might at least have used my son for what he is worth! Wouldn't it be more advantageous, more useful for the Church to have him work as an intellectual?!"

"There are things," I replied, "we cannot understand by mere intellect and common sense. Only faith can enlighten us. Why did Jesus wish to be poor? Why did he wish to hide his divinity and power and live among us as the least of us? Why the defeat of the cross, the scandal of Calvary, the ignominy of death for him who was life? No, the Church doesn't need one more engineer; she needs a grain of wheat to die in her furrows."

So many things cannot be understood on this earth. Isn't everything around us a mystery?

I can understand why Paul had to give up everything—his way of life, his career—for love of God and love of his brethren. But I also understood the reactions of his mother. Indeed, many would say: "What a pity! Such an intelligent person going to work in the Sahara! He could have built a printing press for making available good literature. He could have . . ." And they would be right too.

It's difficult to fathom the mystery of humanity, which is part of the great mystery of God. There are those who dream of a powerful Church, rich in resources and potential, and there are those who want her poor and weak. There are those who devote their lives to study in order to enrich Christian thought, and those who renounce study for love of God and their neighbor.

That is the mystery of faith!

Paul was not interested in having influence upon men. He was content to pray, to disappear. Others will search other paths and achieve holiness in other ways.

Can I doubt the faith of my mother, who would have desired all riches to be in the hands of the Church, to be used for more effective missions?

And I, her son, quite the opposite: dreaming of a simpler faith, a more deeply-felt poverty, and above all, a vocation founded on the lack of riches. Wasn't I right in a way, too?

It's so difficult to judge! So difficult that Jesus besought us not to try to answer these questions.

But to one truth we must always cling desperately—to love!

It's love which justifies our actions; love must initiate all we do. Love is the fulfillment of the law.

If, out of love, Brother Paul has chosen to die on a desert track, by this he is justified.

If, out of love, Don Bosco and Mother Seton built schools and hospitals, by this they were justified.

If, out of love, Thomas Aquinas spent his life among books, by this he was justified.

The only problem is to put into their right perspective these different kinds of "love-in-action." And here Jesus himself teaches us in an uncompromising way:

"The greatest among you must be as the least, the leader be as one who is a servant."

And again: "A man can have no greater love that to lay down his life for his friends."

CHAPTER 14

Oh, You Who Pass By

THE TRACK TO TAIFET is simply horrible.

In fact, I avoid it whenever possible. I prefer to go a few miles out of my way through Ideles and Irafok, rather than through those impassable gorges. One had to make one's way with pick and shovel through rocky tracks, and afterwards sink into the soft sand of the endlessly winding *oued*.

But this time I had no choice and as I set out I mustered all the courage I had, which wasn't much, after a week of warm southerly wind and the fatigue caused by the extreme changes of temperature between day and night.

As usual, the sky was cloudless, and the sun relentless from eight o'clock in the morning on. But I didn't notice. My only concern was the engine of the jeep which seemed on the verge of giving up and no longer wanted to cooperate when the car sunk into the sand.

And yet I had to go on. Who would have come to my aid on that track?

The previous evening, at the well of Tazrouk, I had taken on all the water possible, but what would happen when that was gone?

What would I do if I were stranded in the desert, the very image of death and perpetual silence?

All my hope lay in that engine, whose throb was so familiar to me and which had never let me down before. But now? Would I succeed in crossing the fourteen miles of the ravine of Taifet, with its soft burning sands, its dry, arid gorges?

Nine o'clock, ten, eleven—after three breaks to let the engine cool down I finally reached sight of Taifet, a tiny village of ex-slaves on the edge of the ravine.

I hurled the jeep forward over the track, hoping in this way to avoid having to try to get the wheels to grip the soft sand. The heat was suffocating, and the water was boiling in the radiator.

Then, in a last attempt to keep up the pace, the engine gave one last groan and stopped. The jeep sank down into the sand. I got out of the car, although I was afraid of sunstroke. I didn't have the energy to take the shovel to free the car from the sand. I looked for a little shade. In the *oued,* here and there, were etel bushes, I sought the nearest one and threw myself on the ground in its shade.

I don't know why but at that moment I remembered the prophet Jonah, sitting under the ivy which protected him from the sun while Ninevah burned.

But I had little time for such Biblical reflections because I went to sleep almost at once.

I awoke slowly to the sound of people talking in low voices interspersed with bursts of laughter. I was bathed

in sweat and my head ached. I opened my eyes and saw around me men from Taifet, looking at me and smiling. How white their teeth were, how their dark skin glowed! There were a score of them, and they had interrupted their work on my arrival. Under the etel they had already prepared the fire for tea. The warmth of the beverage restored me.

They invited me to eat with them, and I offered them everything I had on the jeep. The tobacco, particularly, made them talkative. A pleasant interlude followed, but it was so short! They had to get on with their work. And what work!

They had dug in the ravine a subterranean canal called a *fogara,* which would collect the water in which the sand was soaked like a sponge, and conduct it to the nearby fields. There the grain which had been sown was by now fully grown and very thirsty. The usual unpredictable sandstorm had destroyed the old *fogara* and they had to make another without delay. If they were late, even by a week, it could be enough to ruin the harvest, which would mean hunger for the rest of the year.

I offered to work with them for a few days, although I knew my help was not worth very much.

And so I lived for a week with one of the poorest human groups on earth. Work began at dawn, and lasted until sunset.

With primitive tools we dug the tunnel which ran about three yards beneath the surface of the *oued.*

The man working in the tunnel had the advantage of suffering less from the heat, but it was nevertheless an uncomfortable position to work in; working outside one suffered backache less, but the heat was suffocating. In either case it was very arduous and one longed for the evening, for food and rest.

In the evening we ate around the fires and if any dieticians had been present, they could easily have calculated that the calories consumed were well below the vital minimum. It was a small compensation, however, to be able to eat things which were rare for the European taste and palate.

The first evening we were served a little *couscous* with a dish of roasted grasshoppers. The next day came sand mice called *gerboise;* at another time a big firefly called *dobb;* this was very tasty and contained—according to the Tuareg—forty precious medicaments.

At night, wrapped up in a blanket near the huts, I used to gaze at the sky before going to sleep.

What connection could there possibly be between that glittering mass of stars and the misery among which I had fallen; between that infinity of space in the cosmos, and the needs of these mortal men?

This was the mystery of evil, of suffering. The mystery of men who die of starvation, who live, robbed of human dignity, condemned to a life in which the perpetual anguish of trying to find a little bread poisons the joy of the daily sunrise.

But I was too tired to think of why God didn't intervene since he is so powerful and so good. I sought a scapegoat in the "gods" of the earth, the men who could so easily have helped.

What would it cost to write a letter to my friends in Italy? They might immediately have sent me a bulldozer to dig out the trench in a few days. At least they could send me great cement tubes to make the trench stable and secure, and stop it caving in when water first ran into it. And there I was, just sitting motionless and looking at the stars!

Was I justified, just lying there and reflecting in this way?

What use could my poor hands possibly be with so much work to be done?

Wouldn't it be better to look elsewhere for help? This is a question I have often asked myself: so often, in fact, that it has even forced me to question the basis of my vocation.

And yet, faith must be the guide and not common sense.

The common sense of Brother Paul's mother, who could not understand her son's "useless" sacrifice on the Saharan tracks; my own common sense which made me try to convince myself that I would be more use to the people of Taifet if I went away in search of materials for their trench; the common sense of those who believe that one can solve everything with money and that to share people's suffering is simply a waste.

But is the Gospel common sense? Or is it mystery?

When Jesus came on this earth, he, the All-Powerful, he who was love, could he not perhaps have healed all the sick, fed all the hungry, healed all the wounded, raised all the dead?

He raised Lazarus and Jairus' daughter and the son of the widow of Nain, it is true, but only in order to prove that he did not intend to raise all the others—and there were many of them.

This is why, for one who suffers, theology is not enough. Something more is necessary.

When I left for Africa to become a Little Brother of Jesus I lived for some time in Algiers, as the guest of an old friend.

I was very unsettled in those days, and the world appeared to me under quite a new light. It had something to do with that intuition born in the heart of him whom I now wanted to follow along the desert tracks, Charles de Foucauld.

The perspective of a European, materially and culturally endowed, desirous of giving and doing something for others, had turned somersault in me. I would have liked to hide, without money in my pocket, dressed as an Arab, among the anonymous crowd of poor Moslems seething in the alleys of Kasbah.

I remember that around midday I noticed a long string of men in rags lining up near the convent, whose walls were as solid as a fortress. Each man had a tin can. I saw a door open and a nun in a white habit appear; nearby was an enormous smoking pot. It was time for the daily distribution of alms, and each man received his share along with a loaf of bread and warm soup.

I stared at that procession as though in a dream; as I watched those men and women branded with misery, tears ran down my cheeks, so that I could no longer see the bright sky above the African city.

I tried to find a place for myself. I had left my native land, urged on by the desire to give up everything in order to give myself to God among all this poverty; to search out among the poor the crucified face of Jesus, to do something for my wretched and despised brethren, so that, by loving them, I might deepen my union with God.

What was I to do then? Was I to open dispensaries and give bread, medicine and education to these poor people. What was my place in the great evangelizing work of the Church?

I tried to learn from him who had drawn me to Africa, Charles de Foucauld. Quite small, quite humble, tin can in hand, I found him in my imagination, at the end of the queue. He was smiling faintly, as if he wanted to ask pardon for adding himself to the number of the deprived and underpriviledged.

Undoubtedly, at that moment, in spite of my fear of suffering, my reluctance to bear the burdens of others, my fear of taking up the cross, I understood that my place, too, was there, amid the ragged poor, mixing in the mob.

Others in the Church would have the task of evangelizing, building, feeding, preaching. The Lord asked me to be a poor man among the poor, a worker among workers.

Yes, above all, worker among workers, since the world of today was no longer in search of alms as in the time of Francis of Assisi, but a world in search of work, justice and peace.

The world towards which I was journeying was the world in which real poverty is experienced. For people in that world, work is their sackcloth, but they have not chosen it; moreover it is painful, dirty, and poorly paid.

After a week spent at Taifet I left again for Tamanrasset. I felt that I could not bear that wretchedness and poverty any longer. In this I was poorer than those poor men, for I had been unable to bear what they had always borne.

I needed prayer. I longed to find myself alone in my hermitage where Jesus was exposed day and night, in order to unburden myself to him, beseech him, lose myself in him.

Above all I wanted to ask him to make me smaller, emptier, more transparent—and to enable me to return to Taifet.

Yes, return to Taifet to live the last years of my life. Have a little hut "like them," no possessions but a mat and a blanket, "like them," on the shore of that *oued;* drag a little water from it with those *fogaras* which were continually breaking down as though laughing at our labor!

But also to have Jesus in the Host, hidden in the hut; to adore him, pray to him, love him, and obtain from him the strength not to rebel, not to curse, but to accept lovingly what the day would bring.

And so I pray for the day when on the shore of that *oued* a little etel cross will rise like a sentinel to watch over the solitude of those men as they wait, wait for others to come and love them and help them to love.

CHAPTER 15

The Revolt of the Good

THE FACT THAT MY vocation leads me to seek the lowest place means absolutely nothing. What counts is forcing myself to stay in that place every day of my life. And that is terribly difficult.

At the bottom of the human heart there is an ulcer which grows with the years. It is the ulcer of resentment at being exploited by others. Nobody escapes it; it takes time for the soul to locate it and, if and when God wills, to root it out.

Take a family situation. The burden of work is often ill-distributed; one member of the family bears most of the burden. Most often it is the mother.

As the shoulders of one person carry most of the weight, the rest of the family gets away lightly.

But under those shoulders there's a heart; and in that heart, little by little, an ulcer of resentment develops, and grows.

One day, one terrible day, because of some particular incident, serious or trivial, the ulcer bursts and spreads its poison throughout the body.

"I'm putting my foot down! I've had enough! I've been your servant up to now and you haven't even realized. I've sacrificed my life while you enjoyed yourselves," etc., etc.

The same thing can happen in a religious community and then the storm is much greater. Often the very foundations of the community seem in danger of collapse. The poison which is diffused among the members is so strong that it has the power of paralyzing love itself.

And yet that mother is right. She has sacrificed herself for her family. The others have allowed themselves plenty of freedom. She has had no share of it. She has worked, slaved, given up every moment of her day.

But there's something more serious, something which is the real cause of suffering. She hasn't been understood. They have taken her for granted; they haven't, for example, noticed her crying in silence.

Each one of us at this point can tell our own story, and, strangely, we each feel ourselves in exactly the position of that mother: each one of us feels ourselves the victim of someone or something. Someone has had a childhood without affection, another is badly paid at the office, another feels his abilities have not been fully used; someone else hasn't had the promotion he thinks he deserves, another hasn't been understood by his bishop, another has been forced to resign as chair of his company, and another has been sent to work in the kitchen instead of being appointed superior of the convent!

But strangest of all is that each of us is right to a certain extent.

Of course, in our lives we receive insults and abuse from others, but we rather tend to enjoy being the victim. We like to think that the pain is unbearable, the more so because it seems to affect the roots of our being, our relationship with God and with our neighbor.

How can I love, really love my brother or sister who sees me working day after day and repays me with indifference, and even with derision? How can I feel at ease in a convent where my sisters haven't really taken my personality into account and haven't understood my abilities? Why should I still work with enthusiasm when someone has been promoted who doesn't really deserve it?

In fact, I no longer love; I am unable to. But this inability to love is quite crucial because it leaves me with an enormous feeling of indifference.

Whether I like it or not, love is the aim of my life, the reason for my existence, the only thing that really satisfies me. In fact, since I ceased to love I have known no peace.

During my sleepless nights I feel sapped of energy, tormented by the wanderings of my spirit. I try to pray, but even my prayer has become bitter and senseless to me.

It seems that heaven is no longer interested in me. My cry for justice seems to go unheard. It is as though something has changed in heaven and the canons which governed the old system seem no longer to hold with God.

Until the Incarnation it was exactly like that. But the rule of justice alone was not enough. It was good, it was true, but it wasn't complete. Above all, it didn't express God's dynamism, God's infinity. To someone in this blind alley of sin, the canons of justice and truth were unable to offer salvation. Something else was necessary.

Then Jesus came. And his own received him not. Not only that, but they sent him out into the desert like a scapegoat and rejected him.

All humanity surged round him to strike, spit and revile.

And Jesus, the only truly innocent person, bent his head under the blows. He did not invoke justice, and with his flesh and spirit he paid for the sins of the world.

From that moment was established for once and for all the law of forgiveness, mercy and love, which goes far beyond the bounds of justice.

After Calvary, peace was no longer to operate on the thin blade of truth or in the court of law, but in the torn heart of a God who had become human for us in Jesus Christ.

The era of victimization had ended and with Jesus the reign of the victim was to begin.

The true victim, silent and lamb-like, the victim who accepts to be a victim and destroys the thorns of injustice in the fire of his love.

"The Lord loves a happy giver," Paul was to say. And the victim is the happy giver.

God will be the happy giver in his Christ. His gift of himself is unconditional. He will pardon all sins forever. He will give life again to the tired bones of the sinner, he will transform a prostitute into a Mary Magdalene and an ordinary pleasure-seeker into a Saint Francis.

Life will triumph over death, and spring will find strength and beauty in the dung of the earth itself.

"I have overcome the world," Christ will shout in his sacrifice, and joy will flow again in our anguished heart.

Yes, I too must go beyond justice. To triumph over the sickness of victimization I must go beyond it. Like Jesus and in imitation of him, I must wearily climb again the slope of my pain, and throw myself courageously in the descent towards my brothers and sisters, above all towards those whom the short-sightedness of my sick eyes sees as the cause of my evils.

There is no other solution. There is no true peace and union with Jesus without it. As long as I waste time defending myself I get nothing done and I am not truly Christian; I do not know the depths of the heart of Jesus.

To forgive, really forgive, means convincing ourselves deep down that we merited the wrong done to us. What is more, it is good to suffer in silence. Jesus taught that the beatitude is reserved for those who are *persecuted* for the sake of justice.

What would humankind say if, following Jesus on Calvary, they saw him turn in sudden anger towards a man who had given him a kick and shout: "Do you know who I am?" No, Jesus did not turn upon those who insulted him to defend himself. He didn't flaunt his true identity at the crowd which was crucifying him. Above all, he did not hate them within himself.

The perpetual newness of the love of Jesus is all here. He had taught it so well and Luke understood it so well:

> But I say this to you who are listening: Love your enemies, do good to those who hate you, bless those who curse you, pray for those who treat you badly. To the man who slaps you on one cheek, present the other cheek too; to the man who takes your cloak from you, do not refuse your tunic. (Luke 6:27)

It's unmistakable, the Spirit of Jesus, and unique. Paul, without doubt the best interpreter of this spirit in the depths of the heart of Christ, when he wants to outline the Christian's position before God and the world, says in the epistle to the Philippians:

> And your minds must be
> the same as Christ Jesus:
> His state was divine,
> yet He did not cling
> to His equality with God
> but emptied Himself
> to assume the condition of a slave,
> and become as men are;

> He was humbler yet,
> even to accepting death,
> death on a cross. (Phil. 2:5)

This is a summary of all the virtues and all the perfections. This feeling of Jesus, this desire to lower himself to obey the Father and save humanity, will forever remain the climax of the love of Christ.

That is why truth and justice are not enough and we are invited to go further.

The more we "feel we must" abase ourselves in imitation of Jesus, the more humility will reign in our hearts, and peace flow into our lives.

In these lines lies the secret of sanctity.

CHAPTER 16

The God of the Impossible

AN ACCIDENT IN THE MIDDLE of the desert paralyzed one of my legs. When the doctor arrived—eight days later—it was too late; I shall be lame for the rest of my life.

Stretched out on a mat in the cell of an old Saharan fort, I looked at the marks made by time on the mud wall, whitewashed in lime by the soldiers of the Foreign Legion. The heat made it difficult to think. I preferred to pray. But there are certain moments when prayer is not easy.

I remained silent, trying mentally to take my soul beyond the compounds of my room into the little Arab-style chapel where I knew the Eucharist was. The Brothers were working some distance away, some in the fields, some in the workshop. My leg was hurting terribly, and I had to work up the force to stop my mind wandering. I remembered Pius XII once asking in one of his audiences, "What does Jesus do in the Eucharist?" and he awaited the reply from us students. Even today, after so many years, I do not know how to reply.

What does Jesus do in the Eucharist? I have thought about it often.

In the Eucharist Jesus is immobilized not in one leg only, but both, and in his hands as well. He is reduced to a little piece of white bread. The world needs him so much and yet he doesn't speak. We need him so much and he doesn't move!

The Eucharist is the silence of God, the weakness of God.

To reduce himself to bread while the world is so noisy, so agitated, so confused.

It is as though the world and the Eucharist were walking in opposite directions. And they seem to get further and further from one another.

One has to be courageous not to let oneself be carried along by the world's march; one needs faith and will-power to go cross-current towards the Eucharist, to stop, to be silent, to worship. And one needs really strong faith to understand the impotence and defeat which the Eucharist represents and which is today what the impotence and defeat of Calvary was yesterday.

And yet this powerless Jesus, nailed down and annihilated, is the God of the Impossible, Alpha and Omega, the beginning and the end. As John describes Him in the Apocalypse:

A judge with integrity, a warrior for justice. His eyes were flames of fire, and his head was crowned with many coronets; the name written on him was known only to himself, his cloak was soaked in blood. He is known by the name, the Word of

God. Behind him, dressed in linen of dazzling white, rode the armies of heaven on white horses. From his mouth came a sharp sword to strike the nations with; he is the one who will rule them with an iron sceptre, and tread out the wine of almighty God's fierce anger. On his cloak and on his thigh there was a name written: The King of kings and the Lord of lords. (19:11)

Jesus is God of the Impossible; my powerlessness shows his power; my insignificance as a creature shows his being as the creator.

From Job, in his struggle with his creator, God asked an act of trust, by pointing to the magnificence of creation.

Where were you when I laid the earth's foundations? Who decided the dimensions of it, do you know? Or who stretched the measuring line across it? What supports its pillars at their bases? Who laid its cornerstone when all the stars of the morning were singing with joy? (Job 38:4–7)

Today, a saying of Jesus' in the Gospel impresses me more than this quotation about the power of the creator and the absolute powerlessness of the creature: "It is easier for a camel to pass through the eye of a needle than for a rich man to enter the Kingdom of heaven." (Matthew 19:23)

This expression comes to my mind every time I see a camel on the track, and it makes me smile. If he had said "A horse or an ox . . ." but no, a camel, with that hump! Of course a camel can't be made to pass through the eye of a needle!

To create the firmament is certainly a sign of great power, but to make a camel pass through the eye of a needle seems to me greater still; it's quite impossible.

In fact, to the worried and amazed apostles who exclaimed, "Then it is impossible to be saved," Jesus calmly replied, "What is impossible for man is possible for God."

"For you all things are possible," Jesus was to say to the Father in the prayer of Gethsemane. Omnipotence is an attribute of God's.

The real qualities of my humanity are insignificance, weakness, misery, powerlessness. There must be a meaning to this. One must think about it carefully. Is it possible that sin, which invaded the world soon after our creation and which seems at times so inexplicable, has nothing to tell us about God's omnipotence?

Is it possible that the human weakness we see in old age, sickness and death should be something which simply afflicts us and has no further meaning?

When I think of my evening examinations of conscience, it is always a question of things not done or done badly; I can never list positive things.

And even if I can achieve inner peace for a moment, I still have a deep sense of my inadequacy and wretchedness and I have to admit my incapacity to make my love greater.

The memory of the blanket I denied Kada and the awareness of my being unable to make an act of perfect love keep returning to my mind.

I have experienced the same thing in prayer. Left to myself, with my own strength, I have felt the painful reality that without God's help we cannot say even "Abba, Father."

There are moments when God makes us feel the extreme limits of our powerlessness; then, and only then, do we understand our nothingness right down to the depths.

For so many years, for too many years, I have fought against my powerlessness, my weakness. Often I have refused to admit it to myself, preferring to appear in public with a nice mask of self-assurance.

It is pride which will not let us admit this powerlessness; pride which won't let us accept being inadequate. God has made me understand this, little by little.

Now I don't fight any more; I try to accept myself. I try to face up to myself without illusions, dreams or fantasies. It's a step forward, I believe. And if I had made the step while I was still learning the catechism I should have gained forty years.

Now I contrast my powerlessness with the powerfulness of God, the heap of my sins with the completeness of his mercy, and I place the abyss of my smallness beneath the abyss of his greatness.

I seem now to have reached a means of encountering him in a way I have never known before: a togetherness I had never experienced before, an awareness of his love I had never previously felt. Yes, it is really my misery which attracts his power, my wounds which shout after him, my nothingness which makes him throw himself open to me.

And this meeting between God's totality and man's nothingness is the greatest wonder of creation. It is the most beautiful betrothal because its bond is a love which gives itself freely and a love which accepts. Really, it is the truth of God and humanity. The acceptance of this truth comes from humility, and that is why without humility there is no truth, and without truth no humility.

"He has regarded the lowliness of his handmaiden," said Mary when she saw, accepting her nothingness, the essential love of God and felt her flesh become the dwelling place and nourishment of the Word Incarnate.

How wonderful that Mary's nothingness should attract God's all. What sweetness in her prayer when she recognized that she was at the opposite pole from God, where humility not only becomes the acceptance of love, but is one of its demands.

What peace in her total self-giving to him, accompanied by the contemplative gaze at the greatness and perfection of the loved one.

No more perfect relationship exists, and Mary shows in its most perfect form the absorbent thirst of the soul under God's dew.

Thus, after so many years, I feel I have found the solution to the only real problem we have on earth. I have recognized my powerlessness and this was grace. In faith, hope and love I have contemplated the all-power-fulness of God and this, too, was grace.

God can do everything and I can do nothing. But if I offer this nothing in prayer to God, everything becomes possible in me.

I remember the great rock where I was weighed down by my self-centeredness, closed in my purgatory for having denied Kada the blanket.

Within myself I feel the inability to perform an act of perfect love, following Jesus on Calvary, dying with him on the Cross.

Thousands and thousands of years may pass and my position will not change.

But . . . but what is impossible for me, the rich man in the Gospel, is possible for God! It is he who will give me the grace to transform myself; he will make me able to carry out the impossible and remove the obstacle which separated me from the Kingdom. And so it is a question of waiting, of humble and trustful prayer, of patience and hope.

But the God of the Impossible won't ignore my cry.

CHAPTER 17

The Friendly Night

WHEN I FIRST CAME to the Sahara I was afraid of the night.

For some, night means more work, for others dissipation, for still others insomnia, boredom.

For me now it's quite different. Night is first of all rest, real rest. At sunset a great serenity sets in, as though nature were obeying a sudden sign from God.

The wind which has howled all day ceases, the heat dies down, the atmosphere becomes clear and limpid, and great peace spreads everywhere, as though humanity and the elements wanted to refresh themselves after the great battle with the day and its sun.

Yes, the night here is different. It has not lost its purity, its mystery. It has remained as God made it, his creation, bringer of good and life.

With your work finished and the caravan halted, you stretch out on the sand with a blanket under your head and breathe in the gentle breeze which has replaced the dry, fiery daytime wind.

Then you leave the camp and go down to the dunes for prayer. Time passes undisturbed. No obligations harass you, no noise disturbs you, no worry awaits you:

time is all yours. So you satiate yourself with prayer and silence, while the stars light up in the sky.

Those who have never seen them cannot believe what the stars are like in the desert; the complete absence of artificial light, the vastness of the horizon only seem to increase their number and brightness. It is certainly an unforgettable experience. Only the camp fire with the tea water boiling on top and the bread for supper baking underneath, glows with a mellow light against the sparkling heaven.

The first nights spent here made me send off for books on astronomy and maps of the sky; and for months afterwards I spent my free time learning a little of what was passing over my head up there in the universe.

It was all good material for my prayer of adoration. Kneeling on the sand I sank my eyes for hours and hours in those wonders, writing down my discoveries in an exercise book like a child.

I understood, for example, that finding one's way in the desert is much easier by night than by day, that the points of reference are numerous and certain. In the years which I spent in the open desert I never once got lost, thanks to the stars.

Many times, when searching for a Tuareg camp or a lost weather station, I lost my way because the sun was too high in the sky. But I waited for night and found the road again, guided by the stars.

The Saharan night is not only a wonderful time for repose; it also provides a restful dwelling place for the soul. After the day—with all that light—the soul closes up like a house without windows to have their shutters unhinged by the wind or burnt by the sun.

I shall never forget the nights under the Saharan stars. I felt as if I were wrapped around by the blanket of the friendly night, a blanket embroidered with stars.

Yes, a friendly night, a benevolent darkness with restful shadows. In them the movement of my soul is not hindered. On the contrary, it can spread out, be fulfilled, grow and be joyful.

I feel at home, safe, fearless, desirous only of staying like this for hours; my only worry that of the shortness of the night so avid am I to read within and outside myself the symbols of divine language.

The friendly night is an image of faith, that gift of God defined, "The guarantee of the blessings we hope for and proof of the existence of the realities that at present remain unseen" (Hebrews 11:1).

I have never found a better metaphor for my relationship with the Eternal: a point lost in infinite space, wrapped round by the night under the subdued light of the stars.

I am this point lost in space: the darkness, like an irreplaceable friend, is faith. The stars, God's witness.

When my faith was weak, all this would have seemed incomprehensible to me. I was afraid as a child is of the night. But now I have conquered it, and it is mine. I experience joy in night, navigating upon it as upon the sea. The night is no longer my enemy, nor does it make me afraid. On the contrary, its darkness and divine transcendence are a source of delight.

Sometimes I even close my eyes to see more darkness. I know the stars are there in their place, as a witness to me of heaven. And I can see why darkness is so necessary.

The darkness is necessary, the darkness of faith is necessary, for God's light is too great. It wounds.

I understand more and more that faith is not a mysterious and cruel trick of a God who hides himself without telling me why, but a necessary veil. My discovery of him takes place gradually, respecting the growth of divine life in me.

"No one may see God and live," says the Scripture, in the sense that to see him face to face is possible only for those who have passed beyond death.

On earth such is the light, the infinity of the mystery and the inadequacy of human nature, that I must penetrate it little by little. First through symbols, then through experience, and finally in the contemplation which I can achieve on this earth if I remain faithful to God's love.

But it will be only a beginning, getting the eyes of my soul accustomed to so much light: the process will go on endlessly and the mystery will remain as long as we are dominated by God's infinity.

What is our life on earth, if not discovering, becoming conscious of, penetrating, contemplating, accepting, loving this mystery of God's, the unique reality which surrounds us, and in which we are immersed like meteorites in space? "In God we live and move and have our being" (Acts 17:28).

There aren't many mysteries, but there is one upon which everything depends, and it is so immense that it fills the whole space.

Human discoveries do not help us to penetrate this mystery. Future millennia will illuminate no further what Isaiah said and what God himself declared to Moses before the burning bush, "I am who I am" (Exodus 3:14).

Perhaps the sky was less dark for Abraham and the men with the tents than for modern man; perhaps faith was simpler for medieval poets than present-day technicians. But the situation is the same, and the nature of our relationship with God does not change.

The more we grow in maturity, the more we are required to have faith, devoid of sentiment. But the road will remain the same until the last has been born on this earth.

"This is the victory over the world—our faith" (1 John 5:4).

God asks faith of us and this is the true, authentic submission of the creature to the Creator, an act of humility, of love.

Trust in God; giving praise to the All-Powerful; satisfying our thirst for knowledge in the infinite sea of his Fatherhood; accepting his mysterious plan; entering school to listen to his word; knowing how to wait on him. This is an act of adoration worthy of human beings on this earth.

But if through pride we do not wish to set out on the path of faith, and we turn our backs on divine reality and close our eyes before the witness of the stars, where does it get us? Will our consciousness of the mystery increase? Shall we find more light somewhere else?

Without speaking of God, of the Incarnation of the Word and of the Eucharist, what do we know of the physical world itself which surrounds us? Or what, indeed, happens after death? What of the suffering of the creatures or the purpose of creation?

What we know is little more than nothing; and what little we know is all relative unless we go to first causes.

We should be overcome when each discovery we make seems to proclaim, "Have you only just got there?" The advice of Jesus remains true, "If you do not become little children, you will not enter . . ."

What I have tried to say about faith is valid for everyone. No one can escape this reality. It is a gift of God but it needs effort on our part if it is to bear fruit.

God gives us the boat and the oars, but then tells us, "It's up to you to row." Making "positive acts of faith" is like training this faculty; it is developed by training, as the muscles are developed by gymnastics.

David developed his faith by accepting to fight against Goliath. Gideon exercised himself in faith not only by asking a favorable sign from the Lord through the test of the fleece, but by going into battle with few soldiers against a stronger enemy.

Abraham became a giant in faith by making the supreme act of obedience which demanded of him the sacrifice of his son.

In Paul's letter to the Hebrews we read:

It was for faith that our ancestors were commended. . . . Many submitted to torture, refusing release so that they would rise again to a better life. Some had to bear being pilloried and flogged, or even being chained up in prison. They were stoned or sawn in half, or beheaded; they were homeless and dressed in the skins of sheep and goats; they were penniless and were given nothing but ill-treatment. They were too good for the world and they went out to live in deserts and mountains and in caves and ravines. (Hebrews 11:2, 35–38)

But of all men and women who lived by faith, two reached towering heights.

They lived at the watershed between the Old and New Testaments and were called by God to such a unique and magnificent vocation that heaven was made to wait in suspense for their reply: Mary and Joseph.

Mary became the mother of the Word; she gave flesh and blood to the Son of God; and Joseph must veil the mystery, placing himself at her side so that everyone might believe that Jesus was his son.

For these two creatures the night of faith was not only dark, but also painful.

One day Joseph, engaged to Mary, realizes that she is to give birth to a child which he knows is not his.

Think of the task of convincing one's betrothed that the mystery of that birth is due to nothing less than the power of God.

No reasoning could give Joseph peace and serenity. Only faith.

And it is precisely this faith which sustained him, placing him next to the mother of God to accompany her in her destiny and take a full part in her mission.

It won't be easy to follow the example of such a man destined to suffer, the spouse of a woman who is to be called the Mother of Sorrows.

The Baby is born.

A few angels came, it is true, to chase away a little of that darkness, but at once the sky closed on a yet greater darkness. The children of the entire village are slain on account of their Baby, and Joseph and Mary, fleeing, hear the cry and lament of the women of Bethlehem.

Why? Why is the All-Powerful silent? Why doesn't he kill Herod? But this is the point: it is necessary to live by faith. Flee into Egypt, become exiles and refugees, let cruelty and injustice triumph. And so it will be until the end of time.

God didn't soften the path of those whom he put beside his Son. He asked of them a faith so pure and uncompromising that only two souls could live up to this demand.

What an adventure, to live for thirty years in a house where God lived in the flesh of an earthly man; to eat with him, listen to him speak, see him sleep, see the sweat on his brow, and on his hands the calluses of weariness and work.

And all this quite simply, as something normal and everyday; so normal that absolutely nobody will unveil the mystery or realize that the carpenter's son is the Son of God, the Word made flesh, the new Adam, heaven and earth.

My God, what great faith!

Mary and Joseph, you it is who are masters of faith, perfect examples to inspire us, correct our course and support our weakness.

Just as you were beside Jesus, you are still beside us to accompany us to eternal life, to teach us to be small and poor in our work, humble and hidden in life, courageous in trial, faithful in prayer, ardent in love.

And when the hour of our death comes and dawn rises over our friendly night, our eyes, as they scan the sky, may pick out the same star that was in your sky when Jesus came upon earth.